940.8342

D1345209

THE DAY
WAR BROKE OUT

by the same author:

"A Spy Has No Friends."
Baltic-Corner: Travel in Estonia.
Spies At Work.
The Patriot: A novel.
A New Prose Translation of Ovid's *Art of Love*.
Lion With Blue Wings: The Story of the Glider Pilot Regiment.
The Undaunted: The Story of Resistance in Western Europe.
Secret Servants: The Story of Japanese Espionage.
The Art of Spying.
For My Name's Sake: Catholic Resistance to the Nazis and Communists.
Stalingrad—Point of Return: The Story of the Battle.
Two Fleets Surprised: The Story of the Battle of Cape Matapan.
The Fiercest Battle: The Story of Convoy ONS 5.
The Specials: The Story of the Special Constabulary.
Anatomy of Spying.
Petiot—Victim of Chance.
Spy in the Nude: A novel.

for children:

Operation Retriever
Operation Lama
Operation Ormer   The Adventures of Captain
The Spy and the Atom-gun Brian Grant of the
Rockets on Moon Island   Secret Service
Smoke Without Fire

The True Book about The Secret Service.
How Spies Work.
How the Resistance Worked.

R. G. Menzies: A biography.
Montgomery of Alamein: A biography.
Sir Archibald McIndoe: A biography.

Four Greek Fairy Tales.

THE DAY
WAR BROKE OUT

The story of the 3rd September 1939

by

RONALD SETH

Neville Spearman Ltd

LONDON 1963

Printed in Great Britain by
Clarke, Doble and Brendon Ltd
for Neville Spearman Ltd
112 Whitfield Street London W1

Contents

List of Illustrations

7

9. *Above*. Herr Kordt, the German chargé d'Affairs, and his staff at the German Embassy in London about to leave for home. (*Radio Times*, Hulton Picture Library)

10. *Below*. Prime Minister Neville Chamberlain acknowledges the crowd's greeting as he leaves No. 10 Downing Street. (Fox Photos)

11. *Above*. A-sign soon to become familiar in every town and hamlet throughout Britain. (Fox Photos)

12. *Below*. Business as usual. The milkman delivers the milk that morning at No. 10 Downing Street. (*Radio Times*, Hulton Picture Library)

Acknowledgements

WHEN THE IDEA of writing the story of *The Day War Broke Out* finally crystallized, I wrote to several national newspapers, and to one or two provincial ones, asking people to send me their memories of that day. Where I had expected a hundred or two, I received almost a thousand.

This great number provided me with an embarrassment of material, and I have had to select only a fraction for use.

The response to a similar letter in leading European and Commonwealth newspapers was also beyond my best hopes.

To all those who took the trouble to write to me, whether I have used their material or not, may I convey my most grateful thanks. I would have liked to have done so individually, but the great number made this impossible. I hope this acknowledgment will be accepted in this light.

For the historical material in this book, I consulted the following:

King George VI by John Wheeler-Bennet. Macmillan.
Old Men Forget by Duff Cooper. Hart Davis.
Mackenzie King of Canada by H. Reginald Harvey. Oxford University Press.
Jan Christian Smuts by J. C. Smuts. Cassell.
Ciano's Diaries. Heinemann.
Memoirs by Cordell Hull. Hodder and Stoughton.
Australia in the War 1939-1945. Hasluck.
The Fateful Years by Hugh Dalton. Muller.
The Second World War by Winston S. Churchill. Cassell.
Fullness of Days by Lord Halifax. Collins.
Lost Victories by Field Marshal von Manstein. Methuen.
In the Thick of the Fight by Paul Reynaud. Cassell.

9

Panzer Leader by Field Marshal Guderian. Michael Joseph.
The Rise and Fall of the Third Reich by William L. Shirer. Secker and Warburg.

1

Overture

ON THE AFTERNOON of 2nd September, 1939, a young Englishman and a young Canadian were strolling under the still, cloudless skies of the Kadriorg, the English-style park which Peter the Great had planted as the setting for a miniature palace he had commissioned the Italian architect Nicolo Michetti to build on the southern shores of the Gulf of Finland, on the outskirts of Reval, the capital of the province of Estonia, as a summer retreat for his beloved wife Catherine.

The Kadriorg Palace was now the official residence of the President of the Republic of Estonia, and the Englishman was Lecturer in English at the University of Tallinn, as Reval was now called, the Canadian Lecturer in Economics in the same University. Behind them strolled their wives, and about them ran the three-year-old son and eighteen-month-old daughter of the Englishman. The women were talking domesticities, but the men were puzzled, perturbed, on edge.

Again and again they asked one another: 'But why haven't they done anything?' and could only answer their own questions with, 'They must do something!' followed by yet another question, 'Why the long delay? Surely not another Munich?'

The 'They' was the British Government; and what They had to do was declare war on Germany! If They did not do that, the two young men felt that they would never again be able to hold up their heads.

I know this, because I was the Englishman; the Canadian a recently acquired colleague and friend, Arnold Smith.

I had gone to Estonia very early in 1936 with my wife and six-weeks-old son, to take up two appointments in Tal-

11

linn. In the evenings I was to lecture on the English language and literature in the University; in the mornings I was to teach in a large, privately owned co-educational school called the English College.

Estonia, it will be recalled, was a young country as far as independence went. After seven hundred years of varied foreign rule, she had achieved her independence in 1919. Her population numbered a million and a quarter and from the President down to the illiterate peasant in Petseri, ninety-nine per cent of them were staunch Anglo-philes.

Great Britain was the country which, above all others, they had looked to for example; and though they were even further from the British Isles than Czechoslovakia or Austria or Poland, they regarded England, the home of democracy, as the protector of small nations, and of themselves in particular.

At least they had done so—they still did, indeed, though with the direst misgivings to which they dare not confess—until a year ago, when Munich had shaken them, as nothing else had done in the history of their independence.

I do not think that anyone who did not experience living in a small country, defiantly proud of its independence, but weak in the power to protect itself from aggression, could fully appreciate what it meant to an Englishman to see the effect that the betrayal of Czechoslovakia had on people whose regard and respect for his own country was almost as strong as his own pride in his citizenship. For not only was Czechoslovakia betrayed at Munich; so was every peace-loving state too small to protect itself from the predatory maw of a giant, war-like people obsessed by increasing its living-space.

I had come to love Estonia and her people in the two short years I had lived and worked there before Munich, only a little less than I loved England. Immediately after Munich, our friends said little, but there was that unhappiness, that anxiety in their eyes which the shock of disillusionment at betrayal by an admired friend put there; and it hurt me personally to see it there, for I was unable to say, 'I assure you there will be no more Munichs.'

12

Indeed, Munich did not betray merely Czechoslovakia and the small states; it betrayed people like me whose work was, quietly, but as effectively as we could, to communicate the greatness and the honesty of England. Actually the first shock had been administered by the rape of Austria in February 1938, but it had only been a small shock, for the majority of Estonians could understand that the German-speaking Austrians were some sort of special case. In the intervening months the shock wore off a little.

But the greater shock of Munich revived the shock of Austria, though the Estonians were still reluctant to believe that England would no longer champion democracy wherever democracy was threatened.

Then, on 12th March, 1939, this fact was driven home, when Hitler, tearing up the agreements of Munich, marched into Czechoslovakia at six o'clock in the fast breaking eastern dawn.

That morning, as I went into the staff room of the English College, a sudden silence fell on the twenty or so members of the staff gathered there. There was no greeting of *'Tere hommikut, Härra Seth,'* no *'Tervist, Härra Lektor,'* no reply to my greetings, no held out hands to shake, but a silent concentration of attention on books and notices, until Härra Kasements, the deputy principal, an admirer of Britain almost without equal, came into the room, and on seeing me, said, with his eyes sparkling with tears, 'So, Hitler's got the better of your Old Man With the Umbrella again! Next it will be Danzig, then Poland, then Lithuania, Latvia and us, unless the Russians decide to come here first!'

I think I murmured, 'I'm sorry,' but fortunately the bell rang for assembly, and I excused myself from going down. Alone in the staff room, I tried to collect my thoughts. What could I say to these loyal friends?

There was nothing adequate, and I decided to remain silent.

When, on Good Friday, Mussolini marched into Albania, and drew only verbal protests from the Cabinet room of 10 Downing Street, the cynicism which had been conceived by the seizure of Czechoslovakia, came to full term. It was

13

in the eyes and in the voices of all Estonians I knew, whenever England was mentioned; and I took the criticism it embodied to be a criticism of me.

I think I had some justification for acting in this way. On the evening of 12th March, when I had gone into the lecture room allotted to me at the University, instead of the customary crowded benches, the room was empty. Usually, those who attended my courses were waiting for me on the hour.

The silent rebuffs of the morning still hurt, and as I stood on the rostrum surveying the deserted banks before me, my heart turned cold. This is no figure of speech. In the middle of my torso where I have always been led to believe my heart to be situated, there was a physical constriction which made me shiver. It was as though a giant arrow-head of ice had pierced my chest, anaesthetized my heart, and was slowly mixing its freezing moisture with my warm blood.

After some moments, during which I tried to pull myself together, I stood supporting myself by the desk; and as I stood there a young man came in. He was one of my keenest pupils, the type of student who keeps his instructors continually on their toes unless any slipshoddiness that may have crept into their work is to be revealed in all its ugliness.

'What's happened?' I asked him.

'I'm sorry, Härra Seth,' he said. 'They have voted not to attend your lecture today as a protest against what has happened in Czechoslovakia.'

'They think I am responsible?' I smiled at him, though I felt less like smiling than weeping.

'Not personally responsible,' he replied, 'But you are an Englishman, and England is, you must admit, responsible . . .'

'With France,' I reminded him.

'The students have also boycotted the French courses today.'

I was a young man, twenty-six years old, deeply concerned with the dignity of my position. I had been a schoolmaster in England for some time before I had come to Estonia, and held such views of discipline that had a class of boys be-

14

haved in this way, I should have taken such action which would have made them amenable to discipline in future, whatever I required of them.

Fortunately, I had enough sense to realize that I could not cope with the present situation in the same way that I would have dealt with rebellion among a class of English boys. On the other hand, I could not go home and shrug the whole thing off, for, as I saw it, this was not only an affront to me personally, but to my status as an Englishman.

It would be useless, I decided, to demand that the students should came to the auditorium. They would undoubtedly refuse, and their refusal would leave me with no alternative but to report what had happened at once to the Rector. It might come to this eventually, but I hoped not.

I asked where my students were now, and was told that they were in one of the students' common rooms. I went there. As I opened the door, I heard a buzz of voices which indicated that tempers were too roused to allow an orderly discussion to take place without leadership.

I stood in the doorway until one or two students caught sight of me and drew the attention of others to me, and gradually all the talking stopped and we stared at each other.

'Who is the senior man here?' I asked in English.

It took a few seconds to establish who he was, but presently one man accepted the *rôle* and asked me abruptly what I wanted.

'May I have your permission to come in for a few moments?' I asked.

My question took them somewhat by surprise. I did not know that if a member of the teaching staff had cause for entering a student common room, he merely entered.

Again there was a pause, and then the spokesman said, 'Yes, you may come in, please.'

The natural good manners of the Estonians prompted them to make way for me, and I went and stood over by the spokesman. They remained quiet, waiting for me to speak.

'I understand,' I said, 'that you are boycotting my lectures today as a protest against what has happened in Czecho-

15

slovakia. Personally I cannot see the logic in this. I am teaching you the English language and, I hope, something about English literature. However, I am quite prepared to discuss with you any grievance you think you may have.'

The spokesman said, 'We have nothing against you personally, Härra Lektor. Because we have not come to your lecture it is only a gesture, a sign of how we feel.'

'I shall be very happy to hear all about how you feel,' I replied, 'but I believe this is a common room. If we hold our discussion here we may be preventing other students from using the room. May I suggest that we go to the lecture room and have our discussion there?'

This was agreed to. At least I had got them into the lecture room, and I had also gained a certain superiority, for from my place on the rostrum I could dominate them physically.

'Now,' I said, when all were settled. 'Who will begin?'

A student stood up and began to speak in Estonian. I held up my hand and stopped him.

'I am sorry,' I said, 'but I can only listen to what you have to say if you speak in English. My Estonian is not yet so good as your English, and I may misunderstand you.'

There were a few muttered protests, but everyone who stood up made an attempt to say what was in his mind in English. Every mistake in grammar I corrected, sometimes going to the blackboard to do so, and presently note-books came out and pencils moved rapidly over them.

After the second speaker had sat down, I was asked to reply. I told them that I would wait until all had spoken, and then would reply. So, one after another, they rose and said their piece, as if they were representatives of one side in a debate.

Five minutes before the period was up, I indicated I would reply.

'If I were at home in England,' I said, 'I would have said all that you have said. Under a democracy, the right to free speech permits me to voice without hindrance or fear of the consequences disagreement with the acts of my Government.

'But here in Estonia, I am a foreigner. I am sure you will appreciate that loyalty to one's fatherland prevents one

16

from saying anything bad about one's country or Government, however much one may disagree. I cannot, therefore, say to you now, "Yes, I agree with all you have said. My country has betrayed the small nations. My country is being selfish. My country has lost its courage. My country's Government is a bad Government." Would you say such things to me about Estonia if we were in London?'

Nobody spoke, but I could see that my point had been taken.

'What I suggest you should do,' I went on, 'is to draw up a written account of your views, and send them to the British Chargé d'Affaires.'

There were a few murmurs of assent.

Then I smiled. 'Well, time is up. In my view this has been one of the most useful English lessons we have ever had,' I said, and left the rostrum.

I gave two other lectures that evening, and attendance was normal. Some attempt was made to draw up a statement of views, but it came to nothing, and very soon, though Czechoslovakia was not forgotten, I was shown no more marks of disapproval. In any case, the Estonians were too kind a people to bear personal grudges; they were incapable of forming a hatred of individuals such as those Frenchmen are capable of who detest 'perfidious Albion' and look upon every Englishman as the personification of Albion. In my personal relationships I was shown the same friendliness and affection which I had come so much to appreciate. There was no repetition either of boycott, nor of the scene in the staff room of the English College when I had entered it in the morning.

Nevertheless, though I was grateful for this, I had black moments when, on my own, I considered the strange behaviour of my country's leaders. I was perplexed and worried.

At the Legation the official line was taken, and I got no comfort there. Even privately, my acquaintances among the Legation staff brushed off any attempt I made to find out if there were some deep but redeeming motive which I was not clever enough to discern for myself.

17

Two things happened thereafter which put a little heart into me—the guarantee to Poland and the introduction of conscription in England. I took the latter to mean that England fully intended to honour her guarantees to Poland; that there would not be another Munich.

But I found, too, that some of the Estonian cynicism had brushed off onto me, for occasionally I found myself thinking, 'It could be only a gesture in the circumstances, an attempt to make Hitler believe that we mean business next time. But if it comes to a next time?'

Perhaps I ought to explain my personal position. The University of Tallinn was 'nationalized', and I was, therefore an employee of the Estonian Government so far as my lectureship was concerned. The English College was a private school, owned by a remarkable woman, Madame Torvand-Tellmann. I was also an assistant editor of *The Baltic Times*, an English-language weekly, and under-cover organ of the Estonian Government. In addition I was a regular broadcaster for the Estonian State Radio.

I had been appointed to these posts—with the exception of the English College—by the Estonian Government, that is to say, no British body—neither the Legation nor the British Council—could claim part of my allegiance. So far as they were concerned, I was a private Englishman working for a foreign Government. In making the reply that I made to the University students, I was behaving, I think as any Englishman would have done in a foreign country who was motivated by some feelings of patriotism, yet every word the students had said to me that evening I had agreed with, and I realized that my own reaction was much akin to theirs. All this being so, while I could not openly criticize the Government of my country, I felt free to do what I could quietly to counteract its actions which I believed to be wrong. For this reason, during the ensuing months, and particularly after the spring of 1939, I undertook certain assignments for my employers in direct opposition to my own Government's policy.

It came about in this way. My work on *The Baltic Times* and certain other work I did for various Government departments in Tallinn, brought me into direct contact with some members of the Estonian Government, notably the Foreign Secretary, Karl Selter.

It will be recalled that in the spring of 1939, a British Mission had been sent to Moscow to arrange an agreement with the Soviet Government. The Baltic States were involved in the terms of this agreement, for Stalin, believing he saw through Hitler's plans, and that the Führer intended to encircle Russia, was insisting that such an agreement could only be reached if it included provisions for Russian bases in the Baltic States, should Hitler make any move to the East.

I shall never forget the first occasion on which I became aware of the demands Stalin was making. We had among our friends a family of White Russians, a mother and daughter, who had fled to Tallinn at the Revolution. They were members of the Orthodox Church, and as such fasted quite rigidly throughout Lent and then indulged in a period of feasting and parties from midnight on Easter eve throughout Easter week.

On Easter Tuesday 1939, they gave a party to which we were invited, and among our fellow guests was a certain Prince Wolkonsky, a member of the famous Russian family of that name, also a refugee and then working in the Estonian Foreign Office. (He lived, as a matter of fact, with his wife and aged mother—I imagine one of the most formidable of all the Princesses Wolkonsky—in the flat next to ours). As I recall, the party began at six o'clock in the evening—though we knew by now that we should not be expected to leave until the small hours of the following morning—and by seven o'clock all the guests except the Wolkonsky's had arrived.

Their absence raised no comment at first, but when, around half past eight, the young Princess arrived and said that her husband apologized but he was delayed at the Foreign Office, there were speculations in corners and increasingly worried looks on the faces of the men guests.

It was nearly ten o'clock when Prince Wolkonsky did at last arrive, and whether he announced it specifically, or whether he merely implied it, it was soon general knowledge

19

among us that that very afternoon a firm demand for bases on Estonian territory had arrived from the Foreign Office in Moscow.

The effect of the news was terrifying to us who were not very well acquainted with the mercurial temperament of the Russian. Men went pale, and women wept and wailed. Appetites disappeared, wine and vodka were in constant demand. At midnight my wife and I slipped away. I personally felt that we were committing some indecent act in observing this frightening display of emotions.

It is true that if the Russians did come to Estonia, even though they might strictly observe conditions which confined them to their bases, these refugees could no longer consider themselves safe from Communist enmity. They had lost everything once, and had built here in Estonia new lives which it seemed certain would be threatened if the Soviet Union gained a foothold in Estonia. Looking back now, the fear of these people was fully justified; but then it seemed to me that they were allowing themselves to be the victims of exaggeration. At the same time, however, I was perturbed, not on account of the White Russians, but on account of my friends the Estonians; nor have I forgotten the fear that a political expedient can genuinely engender in the hearts of innocent people.

University and school terms finished on 31st May, and the new session did not start until October. Our flat had become too small for our growing family, so we had signed a lease for a new flat, then building, but to be ready by mid-August, and had taken a cottage for the summer in a tiny fishing-village on the north coast.

Arnold Smith and his wife, who had arrived in Estonia shortly before Easter under the auspices of the British Council, had taken over our flat. Smith, besides lecturing at the University was editor of *The Baltic Times*.

The pressure which the Soviet Government continued to apply throughout the summer and the Estonian Government's reactions to it was faithfully reflected by Smith in the newspaper. To the Russian request for bases the Estonians returned an unequivocal no, until the question of Estonian bases became, so it seemed, the thread by which hung the signing of an Anglo-Soviet Treaty. The House of Commons backed the Tallinn Government, Chamberlain himself proclaiming that the British Government would never exert pressure upon the Estonians to give way, and the Estonian attitude was crystallized in one of Arnold Smith's headlines —a quotation from a statement by Karl Selter—'There are no Hachas here,' Hacha being the treacherous Slovak leader who had made Hitler's task in occupying Czechoslovakia so much easier.

During that wonderful summer, I had resigned from my post on *The Baltic Times* so as to be completely free from any kind of encumbrance—I was employed in a special confidential capacity by the President (who was also the Chief Executive). The *rôle* I played I must leave for another account, but it brought me into direct contact with the Anglo-Russian negotiations. The climax of this work came towards the end of August, when I carried a private communication to our own Foreign Secretary, Lord Halifax. Halifax's reaction to my message revived all my old fears.

The pronouncements in the House of Commons and elsewhere, had comforted me a little. I think I was motivated as much by wishful-thinking as I was by conviction that the British Government meant what it said. My Estonian friends, who came to our cottage at week-ends to see us, were sceptical, and there were times when I lost patience with them, but after my visit to London I had a terrible feeling that I had wronged them.

I had to return to Tallinn to adjudicate in University entrance examinations. As our new flat was not ready, the Directress of the English College, Madame Torvand-Tellmann, allowed us to use her town flat, as she was still at her country house, a few kilometres outside Tallinn.

We arrived back in Tallinn on 23rd August, to the bombshell of the Molotov-Ribbentrop Pact. In Estonia, the signature of the Pact was taken to mean that a German attack on Poland was merely a matter of time, and everywhere I went I was met with the same question, 'Will England fight if Poland is attacked?'

21

Despite their cynicism, the Estonians desperately needed reassurance. Even if they did not believe it in their hearts, outwardly they had to have something to cling to, for if Poland went under, the overwhelming chances were that their turn would be next, either to Germany or Russia.

I sensed this, and told them firmly, 'Yes, without doubt!' But my reply was as much to bolster my own doubts and fears. In order to hang on to my fast-waning courage, I had to convince myself that at last England meant what her leaders proclaimed; and for a short time I did convince myself.

On 1st September, Hitler marched against Poland.

I had expected an immediate declaration of war by England and France.

But when Arnold Smith and I and our wives were strolling on that Saturday afternoon in Kadriorg Park, thirty-six hours had elapsed since the first shots had been fired, and there had been no declaration of war.

In those thirty-six hours I had received many taunts from Estonian friends. I had called on Karl Selter, the Foreign Minister, to discover whether he had any idea of what was happening, because a call at our Legation had met with an official denial that they knew anything. Selter told me in strict confidence, that reports from London seemed to indicate another Munich. I could not and would not believe him; yet as the hours slipped by and no news came, I began to be terribly afraid.

Arnold Smith was no wiser. He, too, was worried and perplexed.

'Yes, they must do something!' he echoed me, as we sauntered under the spreading chestnuts and limes and among the formal flower-beds of the Palace gardens.

If only we had known what had been happening!

*   *   *

The impending signature of the Molotov-Ribbentrop Pact had been announced on the evening of 22nd August.

The Italian Foreign Minister, Mussolini's son-in-law,

22

Count Galeazzo Ciano, was on the eve of going to meet Ribbentrop at the Brenner Pass to acquaint the German Government with the fact that Italy would not support Germany in any steps Hitler might decide to take. Contrary to Ribbentrop's way of thinking at the beginning of August, Mussolini was, at moments, quite convinced that France and England would go to war if the Nazis marched against Poland. But Italy was quite unprepared for war, and at first the Duce was anxious to adopt a policy of neutrality to give himself time to get prepared.

During the next few days he changed his mind again and again. On 7th August he felt impelled to honour his agreements with Hitler, though he resented the cavalier way in which the Führer had been treating him recently.

On 15th August, he was for acting independently of Germany; on the 17th, he was for declaring war; on the 18th, he thought France and Britain would *not* go to war; on the 19th he was for declaring Italian neutrality; on the 20th, he would join Germany, as he was afraid of Hitler's anger if he did not. On 21st August, he urgently recalled Ciano, who was visiting Albania, so that the Count might meet Ribbentrop and tell him that Italy would remain neutral, and Ciano arranged to meet the German Foreign Minister at the Brenner Pass.

At ten-thirty that evening, Ribbentrop telephoned that he would prefer to meet Ciano at Innsbruck rather than at Brenner, as he was on his way to Moscow to sign a political pact. Mussolini, taken aback by this first news of negotiations between his Axis partner and their old enemy, Russia, decided that Ciano's visit to Ribbentrop was no longer timely.

The Duce, like everyone else, appreciated the significance of this Pact, and was not surprised when, on 25th August, Ribbentrop told Ciano that Polish provocation was increasing and that Hitler was determined to put an end to it quickly.

This news made Mussolini change his mind once more; he would stand by Hitler. Ciano, however, managed to convince him that Italy could not go to war unless Germany supplied a vast list of arms and other essential supplies, and the Duce agreed that he should inform the Germans of this. The Nazis asked for lists, but soon returned answer that they could supply only a very small fraction of the requirements. Faced with this refusal, Mussolini saw that he must remain neutral for the time being.

Hitler appreciated the Duce's position, but requested that the announcement of Italy's neutrality should be delayed as long as possible. That was on 26th August. In the meantime, Hitler had been increasing the pressure on the Poles, which was to come to a head three days later.

The British Government had also read the signs and the Prime Minister had immediately given orders for the recall of Parliament. On 31st July, as the summer Parliamentary recess approached, the Opposition had criticized the Government for taking no steps to keep Parliament sitting in view of the dangerous international situation, and moved an amendment that Parliament should meet again in three instead of the eight intended weeks, to which 'rebel' Conservatives, led by Winston Churchill, Leo Amery and others, and by the Liberal leader, Sir Archibald Sinclair, gave their support.

Unfortunately, Arthur Greenwood, who was leading the Opposition owing to the absence through illness of Mr. Atlee, made a reference to a similar situation which had occurred during the early stages of the Czech crisis the year before. Whereupon Chamberlain, who was going to Scotland to fish, made the vote on the adjournment one of confidence, and though he received a majority—much smaller than any previous majority in the life of the Government—there was much ill-feeling among many who voted for him.

Besides recalling Parliament at once on receiving news of the German-Russian Pact, Chamberlain also wrote to Hitler, telling him that the conclusion of the Pact would not deflect the British Government from fulfilling its pledges to Poland. A statement was also issued in the same terms by the Cabinet.

This statement had appeared in the Estonian Press, and for Arnold Smith and me on 2nd September it made the delay in declaring war all the more puzzling, and certainly gave added weight to Karl Selter's fear that another Munich

24

was being prepared. But to add to our bewilderment and worry, other steps which the British Government had taken in the days immediately following 23rd August seemed to us either the acme of cynicisms or downright dishonesty, and already we were beginning to feel shame.

If there were to be another Munich, I knew that I should not be able to remain in Estonia, for I would never be able to look my Estonian friends in the face again.

Perhaps it was just as well that Arnold Smith and I did not know some of the events that had been taking place in the chancelleries of Europe as we walked in the Kadriorg Park. If we had, we might have been more depressed than we were already. To try to throw some light on our ponderings, we decided to go over what we did know.

For example, we knew that Chamberlain had written to Hitler warning him that Britain would fight if Poland were attacked. We knew that the Cabinet supported him in this. We knew that Parliament had been recalled, and we knew, too, that the King and Queen had returned to London.

King George VI had been holidaying at Balmoral when the news of the Pact became public, and he had decided to return to London at once. He arrived on the morning of 24th August, and immediately began consulting his ministers. The King had looked further afield than many of his advisors had, and had noted the effect that the signing of the Pact had had on the third Axis partner, Japan.

Tokyo had also been taken almost completely by surprise, and first reactions had been unfavourable. The King had an idea that now might be the time to attempt to detach Japan from the Axis, and he suggested to Lord Halifax that he should write personally to Emperor Hirohito as a first step in this direction.

Halifax, who had not studied this aspect of the situation very closely, gave as his opinion that Japan's reactions against the Pact had not been violent enough up to then, to warrant this step, and he advised the King not to write.

The news of the pact had caused a flood of appeals to Hitler from the heads of many Governments, including King Leopold of the Belgians, who spoke for all the small

25

neutral states, the Pope and two from President Roosevelt. The Prime Minister of Canada, Mackenize King, also wrote to Hitler, and on 26th August suggested to Chamberlain that the King should make a direct appeal to the German head of state. The King himself had suggested such an approach during the Czech crisis and had been advised against it, but he was more than willing to do so now. Once more, however, Chamberlain said that he did not think the moment to be suitable, but he would keep the idea in mind. The King never did write.

On 25th August, the British and French Governments had signed military alliances with Poland. This was another fact Smith and I knew. The signing of these alliances had a temporary effect on Hitler, who cancelled his orders for launching the attack on Poland planned for the 26th.

Since the beginning of August, Hitler had been backing his political pressure on the Poles with military measures. German troops had been concentrated on Poland's frontiers, and at the head of them was Colonel-General von Rundstedt, whose Chief of Staff was Major-General Erich von Manstein.

On 19th August, Rundstedt and Manstein had received instructions to meet the Führer at Obersalzburg on the 21st, and on arrival had found that it was a full meeting of all the army and army group commanders and their chiefs of staff, and the appropriate navy and air force leaders. Both Manstein and his chief had taken it to mean that this was to be a serious military conference, but before Hitler took his place at the table, Goering came into the room, looking, according to Manstein, like someone dressed for a fancy-dress ball. The Chief of the Luftwaffe was wearing a white shirt under a green jerkin, grey shorts and long grey silk stockings, and on his feet were a pair of massive laced boots. Round his considerable belly he had buckled a red leather sword-belt richly studded with gold from which hung an ornamental dagger.

On seeing this surprising spectacle, Manstein whispered to his neighbour, General von Salmuth, 'I suppose the Fat Boy's here as strong-arm man?'

Hitler followed Goering almost immediately, and at once launched into his address. His manner and tone were those of a determined man, his mind made up to bring the Polish-German question to a head, even at the price of war. Nevertheless, if the Poles were to give in to German pressure, he would be quite prepared to accept a peaceful solution. He was, however, quite convinced that Great Britain and France would not fight.

Hitler did not allow any discussion to take place, but as a result of the speech, many of the Generals, Rundstedt and Manstein among them, no longer believed that that was inevitable, and that there would be another Munich. They thought this, despite the fact that they were ordered to take up their commands by 24th August.

On 25th August Rundstedt received, at three twenty-five in the afternoon, a message from the High Command: 'Operation Plan White (the code-name for the Polish assault): D-Day—26.8: H-Hour—0430.' For a moment or two, neither Rundstedt nor Manstein could believe it; but everything was ready, and all they had to do was wait.

They were at dinner that evening in Rundstedt's headquarters in the Monastery of the Holy Cross in Neisse, when an urgent message arrived from the High Command by telephone: 'Do NOT repeat NOT commence hostilities. Halt all troop movements. Mobilization to continue. Deployment for Plans White and West to proceed as scheduled.'

Such a counter-order at the eleventh hour can be almost impossible to execute. However, by dint of frantic telephoning, Manstein managed to reach everybody concerned in good time.

Interested to know what had caused Hitler to change his mind, all they could learn was that negotiations were continuing. For the next four days they were to remain in suspense.

What had happened was that Hitler, on receiving Chamberlain's letter of 24th August, had believed that he would get what he wanted without fighting, and he had replied that he wished for a friendly understanding with Britain, but that there must first be a settlement of the differences

27

between Poland and Germany. On receiving this news, the British Prime Minister instructed Lord Halifax to seek assurances from Poland that she was willing to negotiate. If somewhat reluctantly, Poland gave these assurances.

Hitler, no doubt hoping to repeat his success with the President of Slovakia, the execrable Hacha, earlier in the year, ordered the Poles, as he had done the Slovak Government, to send to Berlin a representative who would have full powers to negotiate without having to refer to the Polish Government or Parliament. Warned by Hacha's awful example, the Poles refused to fall into the trap. They told Hitler that Poland was a democracy and that democracies did not operate in that way.

Hitler then presented his infamous Sixteen Points to Poland. This was early on 31st August.

Late on the evening before, Ribbentrop summoned the British Ambassador in Berlin, Sir Nevile Henderson, to him and had read him at break-neck speed the conditions which Germany proposed imposing on Poland. Sir Nevile asked for a copy of the document, and was told that one was not available. Nevertheless, he had heard enough to know that Poland could not possibly accept. Hitler must also have known this.

At all events, at five o'clock in the afternoon of 31st August, he issued a fresh order to von Rundstedt:

'Directive No. 1 for the Conduct of the War.'
D-Day—1st September: H-Hour—0445.

Meanwhile, on 24th August the British Parliament had met and passed through all its stages an Emergency Powers (Defence) Bill, which enabled regulations to be made when the need arose without resort to Parliament. Its powers were soon called upon.

The next day A.R.P. organizations were put on a war footing; Anti-Aircraft defences were fully deployed; some reservists were called up for the Royal Air Force; all service leave was stopped; and on the day that Hitler marched into Poland, the evacuation of women and children from the great cities was ordered; and a black-out was enforced from that evening.

The practical measures for all these things had been fully prepared for some months. Throughout the summer, teachers and others had made lists of children's names, and had done everything they could to make the operation work as smoothly as possible, should it ever have to be set in motion. Despite all their care, however, not everything went according to plan.

Mrs. J. W. Burley, writing to her parents in New Zealand on the evening of 1st September, told them: 'I don't know why, but only about twenty per cent of the children that we expected arrived today. The teachers think that the mothers would not part with them at the last moment. One would think that in the circumstances people would be reasonable. But we are nearly grey-haired with complaints. We put one teacher and his wife and eight-year-old boy into an hotel, and they complain that it is on the main road, and too noisy for the child. Whew! And we have more children and mothers with children under school-age coming tomorrow.'

Helen Dedman, who was headmistress of a junior mixed and infants school in east London at the time, gives another side of the picture. She writes: 'Preparations for the evacuation of school children had been made months beforehand. Lists were prepared in triplicate, one for me, one each for the billeting officer and the education authority in the reception area, wherever that might be. As far as we know we would be setting out into the blue destination unknown.

'There were two hundred and fifty children in my party, ages three to fourteen, and I had to have one helper for the journey to every ten children. I said to the children with great emphasis, "This is your lady and you MUST stay close to her, or you may get lost and no one will know where you are." And children in those days did as they were told.

'When the fateful morning came, we went in a crocodile to Bethnal Green Station, and I could have wept to see the faces of the children bright with anticipation of a train journey and a trip to the country, and the patient quiet mothers letting their children go off into the unknown.'

After a wait of some hours in the school playground next to the station, a train came in for Miss Dedman's party. She goes on: 'In my carriage were ten children, myself and my sister, who was a mother herself and acting as one of my helpers. I had noticed that her rucksack looked very heavy and bulky and as the journey went on I discovered why.

'She had brought a bundle of comics, some towels and two large bottles of water, one for drinking and one for washing. Thanks to the last, our ten alighted with moderately clean faces. We had left school at 11.30 a.m. and at 6.30 p.m. we got to Bury St Edmunds, and were "there".

'We were welcomed by a party of local people under the demand of a very efficient and energetic lady. She gave the order "Line up in fours," and rushed up and down the platform pushing the children into lines of four. But four into ten won't go, and as soon as she had passed, my children, mindful of my instructions, coalesced in tens round their own ladies.

'The other school party, who had travelled in the same train with us, by some accident ranged themselves some to one side of my party and some to the other. The energetic commander-in-chief began to send off the other party in bus loads into the surrounding villages. Soon she was trying to take some of my children in order to complete bus loads. They refused to be parted from their ladies, and, going to the rescue, I suggested that the loads should be completed with more children from the other school first. Finally the C.-in-C. lost patience with me and mine, and said, "This woman won't be parted from her children. They had better all stay in town."

'We were then led to the town billeting station. Here confusion reigned, for the helpers had been told that all the children by this train were to go into the country. All the papers had been packed away and everybody was ready to go home.

'The necessary papers were quickly unpacked and billeting began. Boy Scouts and Girl Guides rushed upon us taking a child in each hand to a billeting officer for allocation to a new home.

'I did my best to get them to keep families together, but often two red-heads or two curly-heads were taken to be brothers and sisters, and, inspite of their protestations to the contrary, were sent off together.'

Eventually, however, all was sorted out, except that all cards to parents, telling them of the new addresses of their offspring, had been packed and were not accessible.

Nor were parents and teachers the only ones to run into difficulties. James Percival had arranged to be married in Manchester Cathedral on 2nd September. Late in the evening of the 1st, he was told that his best-man had been called up.

Right through into the early hours of the following day, he tried to make contact with his friends, only to find that each of them had also been called up. At two o'clock in the morning, wondering whether one could be married unaccompanied by a best-man, he knocked up the last friend he could think of, and with relief heard that he would have a best-man after all.

Similar events had been taking place in France.

As soon as the signing of the Moscow Pact was announced, the Prime Minister. M. Daladier, at the request of his Foreign Minister, M. Georges Bonnet, called together the Ministers for National Defence and the Chiefs of the General Staff in secret conference.

On the following day, 24th August, the Council of Ministers (Cabinet) met, and though no one suggested that France should not honour her pledges to Poland, M. Georges Mandel, Minister for the Defence of the Colonies, proposed that if the Polish-German dispute should result in another Munich, at least Poland should take part, and not be excluded from discussions as Czechoslovakia had been. Everybody agreed with him.

It appears that there was a little desultory general discussion and after Daladier had asked the Council to give him authority to inform the Poles of the necessity to act with moderation, and to commit no hostile act, even if Hitler should annex Danzig. This authority having been given, the meeting broke up.

The Poles, somewhat naturally, were apprehensive of what was happening between London, Paris and Berlin. They felt that, despite the pledges and alliances, they were gradually being manœuvred into a position in which, should they refuse some German demand, the British and French Governments would say they were being unreasonable, and use this to retract their undertakings.

In the meantime, Count Ciano in Rome, was being active. At nine o'clock on the morning of 31st August, Attolico, the Italian Ambassador in Berlin, telephoned him to say that the situation was becoming more and more desperate, and that unless something were done, there would be war in a few hours.

Ciano immediately went to the Palazzo Venezia to see Mussolini to try to find some way to prevent this, and after some discussion the Duce agreed that Ciano should telephone Lord Halifax with the suggestion that if the British Government would agree to the handing over of Danzig to Germany, Mussolini would intervene with Hitler.

'Empty-handed,' said Mussolini, 'I can do nothing. With a fat prize, I may be able to.'

Halifax replied that he would put the suggestion to Chamberlain. Within a short time, Halifax telephoned Ciano to say this proposal was quite unacceptable to the British Government.

Nothing daunted, Ciano returned to Mussolini, who now put forward a new idea—a last attempt to avert disaster. He proposed calling Britain, France and Germany to a conference on 5th September with the object of 'discussing those clauses of the Versailles Treaty which are disturbing Europe.'

Delighted, Ciano summoned the British Ambassador, Sir Percy Lorraine, and the French Ambassador, M. François-Poncet. Both received the proposal enthusiastically, though François-Poncet's enthusiasm was tempered with scepticism.

Had Arnold Smith and I been aware of these moves, I think we would have packed our bags at once.

Both Ambassadors returned to their Embassies and telephoned their respective Foreign Ministers. Within an hour of Sir Percy's speaking to Halifax, he was informing Ciano that the British Foreign Secretary was favourably disposed to the proposal but that he must obviously submit it to the British Government.

Ciano pressed for a quick reply, but had received no word from London when at 8.30 p.m. he was informed that telephonic communications between England and Italy had been cut.

In the French Council of Ministers, Bonnet, the Foreign Minister, saying that he was sure that Great Britain would accept Mussolini's proposal, proposed that France should do likewise. Daladier, the Prime Minister, believed that Britain would only accept it if all mobilization were halted. This would mean France cancelling her mobilization orders, which would not be at all easy to do. After come discussion, it was decided to accept the proposal on condition that Poland should be present at the conference.

Before Ciano could be informed of this, German radio stations were announcing that the attack on Poland was about to begin.

During the last weeks of August, Winston Churchill had been visiting the French front on the Rhine at the invitation of General Georges, commander-in-chief of the north-eastern front. He was deeply impressed by what he saw.

After this visit, he spent a few days painting with French friends, but as the signs became more and more threatening, he decided to return home, and arrived in London on 26th August.

Next day, he received as guest at Chartwell, his country home, General Ironside, who had just returned from a visit to Poland, with glowing reports of the strength, preparedness and courage of the Polish Army.

On 30th August, believing war inevitable and imminent, and that Hitler regarded him as a sufficiently dangerous enemy to have ordered his immediate liquidation by one of the 25,000 Germans who were in England, he called his former Scotland Yard detective, Inspector Thompson, from retirement. He instructed the Inspector to bring with him his

33

pistol, and got out and cleaned his own weapons. That night and for the next few nights, they took it in turns to keep watch against murderous intruders.

The British Minister upon whom a grave responsibility devolved at this time was, naturally, the Minister for War, Leslie Hore-Belisha.

Hore-Belisha had succeeded Duff Cooper at the War Office on the latter's move to the Admiralty in 1937. He had brought about vast changes in the Army and was greatly disliked by the senior blimps. He had, among the many unpopular measures he instigated, introduced conscription for the first time in peace-time, though in time the wisdom of this measure had been accepted by the majority.

He was an extremely able and competent administrator, and a very courageous man. From the moment that the Moscow Pact was announced he urged the Prime Minister to give his consent to the calling-up of 300,000 men of the Territorial Field Army, but Chamberlain would agree only to 35,000 men being summoned.

He was also one of those Ministers who put forward the view that a stiff line should be taken with Hitler. He resisted attempts at conciliation, being quite convinced that Hitler intended war whatever happened, and was equally strongly against negotiations at this point.

On 28th August, he entertained Churchill at lunch, and at 5 p.m., after an A.R.P. practice at the War Office, went to the Palace. The King said he would like to see the War Room at the War Office, and Hore-Belisha made arrangements for a visit next day.

In the evening he again urged Chamberlain to allow him to call out the whole of the Territorial Field Army, but without success.

After attending a Cabinet meeting on the following day, he received the King and the Duke of Gloucester, who stayed at the War Office for about an hour. The King had only just gone, when Arthur Greenwood, who was still leading the Opposition in Mr Atlee's continued absence through illness, arrived to say that the Opposition were in favour of full mobilization immediately while a little later

Lord Halifax telephoned him to tell him that he, too, supported full mobilization, and would add the weight of his advice to Chamberlain on this question.

Next day, Chamberlain gave way to the extent of agreeing to the call-up of 145,000 men of the Army Reserve, and to the beginning of the evacuation of women and children on 1st September, that is, in two days' time.

The 31st August, Hore-Belisha spent the day attending to the implementation of these arrangements, and in the evening, tired and exhausted, went down to his home in the country for the night. There, at 5.30 a.m. next morning, 1st September, the telephone by his bedside rang, and he heard the voice of Lord Gort, Chief of the Imperial General Staff, telling him that the Germans had attacked Poland.

At roughly the same time, the President of the United States was also being awakened by his Ambassador in Paris, William C. Bullitt, with the news of the attack. Roosevelt immediately telephoned the Secretary of State, Cordell Hull, and the Secretaries for War and the Navy, and within the hour the Government of the U.S.A. was on the alert.

Back in England, as soon as he had reached London from the country, Hore-Belisha issued orders for the mobilization of the whole army, while Lord Chatsfield, First Lord of the Admiralty and Sir Kingsley Wood, Minister for Air, issued similar orders to the Royal Navy and the Royal Air Force.

Duff Cooper, who had resigned from the Government as a protest against Munich, and had been in the wilderness ever since, spent the morning of 1st September playing golf at Goodwood. At eleven o'clock he was listening to the B.B.C. news and heard for the first time the Sixteen Points which Hitler had presented to the Poles. He did not yet know that Germany had marched into Poland.

After his round of golf, he was in the bar and overheard some other members, among them the club secretary, discussing the future of racing, and wondering what would happen to the meetings scheduled for the week-end. Duff Cooper asked the secretary who replied, 'Well, Hitler started on Poland this morning, you know.'

He has recorded, 'As we drove back to Bognor, my heart felt lighter than it had felt for a year.'

A telegram was awaiting him, informing him that the House of Commons was meeting that evening, so he returned to London, and later dined at the Savoy Grill with friends, among them Winston Churchill.

Churchill, who had also been in the wilderness far longer than Duff Cooper, had to leave half-way through the meal to see Chamberlain. The Prime Minister had invited him to join the Government as a Minister Without Portfolio and a member of the small War Cabinet which he proposed setting up should war come.

About this time, the Parliamentary Executive of the Labour Party was meeting to consider another Chamberlain invitation—that the Socialists should join the Government. Actually, this was purely a matter of form, for the Opposition had been antagonistic to the Government's handling of Hitler from the beginning to such a degree that it could never have agreed to serve under Chamberlain's leadership. But the matter had to be considered formally, and as everyone expected, the decision taken was the unanimous one to reject the invitation.

At two o'clock on the afternoon of Saturday, 2nd September, the House of Commons began assembling in the expectation of hearing a statement that Great Britain was at war with Germany. (Arnold Smith and I were at the same time taking our walk in Kadriorg Park.) In the event, the Commons were to have a long wait. The Cabinet had not been summoned to meet until four-thirty to discuss the sending of an ultimatum to Hitler.

This situation had arisen because to add to all the other momentous matter which had to be considered on this day, the French Government had asked Ciano to suggest the possibility of a conference to Hitler, though Mussolini had abandoned his plan for calling such a conference as soon as he had heard that Germany had marched into Poland.

Somehow the French and British Governments had to show some kind of a united front. The French had taken their decision without adequately consulting the British Government, which, as soon as it heard what the French were doing, made quite clear to them that they could agree to such a conference only if Hitler withdrew all his soldiers from Polish soil.

Since the first attempt at a blitzkrieg was exceeding all expectations, and Hitler could now see that he could obtain more by carrying on than if he agreed to meet round the conference table, quite naturally he refused to accede to the British condition.

All of which had caused a considerable to-ing and fro-ing, and inevitable delay. Nevertheless, the British Government had, or so it would appear, hardened in its determination to issue an ultimatum that must lead to war should Hitler refuse to withdraw his forces from Poland—with or without a conference—for the Cabinet meeting at four-thirty was merely to discuss the timing of the issue of the ultimatum to the German Government.

However, even this was edged about with yet all kinds of other difficulties, since the French were now urging that there should be a delay of at least forty-eight hours before any ultimatum should be issued, since they needed that time to complete their mobilization.

It must be accepted that because of his other preoccupations on this day, Chamberlain had no time to give further thought to his plans to take Churchill into his Government. Shortly after midnight on the 1st September, within a few hours of his interview with Chamberlain, Churchill had been going over the list of proposed members for the War Cabinet and had come to the conclusion that they were a very old team. He wrote to Chamberlain pointing this out.

'I make out,' he wrote, 'that the six you mentioned to me yesterday aggregate 386 years, or an average of over sixty-four! Only one year short of the Old Age Pension!'

He then went on to suggest that if Eden and Sir Archibald Sinclair, the leader of the Liberals, were added, they would bring the average age down to fifty-seven and a half. He also expressed his misgivings at news he had received from Paris that there was talk of another note being sent

37

to Germany, and expressed the hope that the Prime Minister would be able to announce a declaration of war by England and France at the latest when Parliament met; at the same time pointing out that if Great Britain wished to seize a valuable prize of war, in the shape of the great German liner *Bremen,* which was in British waters, on her way back to Germany, the Admiralty would have to act without delay.

The delaying tactics of the French had not prevented the Prime Minister, Daladier, from announcing in the Chamber of Deputies, 'Poland is our ally. We have given certain pledges to her between 1921 and 1925, and these pledges have been confirmed. I ask the Chamber to vote the necessary credits for the opening of hostilities.' And he had received the vote.

But news of this did not reach the sitting House of Commons. The scene there was to be graphically described by the French Ambassador in London, M. Corbin.

'Whilst the Chamber of Deputies and the Senate were meeting in Paris, the House of Commons was itself sitting,' he has written. 'This time along all the benches of the House an excitement was manifest, which the statements of the Prime Minister did not succeed in calming.'

Chamberlain had eventually entered the House at eight o'clock and had gone immediately to the despatch box.

At the Cabinet meeting, after much discussion, it had been agreed that an ultimatum should be sent to Germany to expire at midnight that night. But when the Prime Minister spoke, all he said was, 'His Majesty's Government will be bound to take action unless the German forces are withdrawn from Polish territory. They are in communication with the French Government as to the time limit within which it would be necessary for the British and French Governments to know whether the German Government are prepared to effect such a withdrawal.'

He made no mention of midnight or any time for the expiry of the ultimatum!

Duff Cooper sat listening to this statement red-faced with

38

mounting anger. He believed, as did many members of all parties, that Chamberlain's statement hinted that even at this late hour, there was going to be another Munich.

Sitting next to Duff Cooper was Anthony Eden, who had resigned in February 1938 over differences with Chamberlain about the latter's treatment of Hitler and Mussolini, and on the other side of Eden sat Leo Amery.

As Arthur Greenwood followed the Prime Minister for the Opposition, Leo Amery called across the floor of the House to him, 'Speak for England!' This cry was taken up in all parts of the House, with variations on the Labour benches such as, 'Speak for the workers!'

Greenwood now retrieved his rather inept handling of the situation on the last day of the previous session which had provoked Chamberlain into demanding a vote of confidence in his handling of the dictators, and rose magnificently to the occasion. In a quiet speech, he made clear how the majority of people in the country were becoming increasingly disturbed by the delay in Britain's honouring her pledges to Poland.

'An act of aggression took place thirty-eight hours ago,' he said. 'The moment that act of aggression took place, one of the most important treaties of modern times automatically came into operation . . .

'It is not for me to rouse any kind of suspicion—and I would never dream of doing so at this time—but if, as the Right Hon. Gentleman has told us, deeply though I regret it, we must wait upon our Allies, I should have preferred the Prime Minister to have been able to say tonight definitely, "It is either peace or war." Tomorrow we meet at twelve. I hope the Prime Minister then—well, he must be in a position to make some further statement . . .'

Here he was interrupted by some Members with, '*Definite* statement,' and he went on, 'And I must put this point to him. Every minute's delay now means the loss of life, imperilling our national interests and the very foundations of our national honour.'

He finished: 'I cannot see Herr Hitler, in honesty, making any deal which he will not be prepared to betray. Therefore,

thinking very hurriedly in these few minutes, I believe that
the die is cast, and we want to know in time.'

Greenwood was followed by Sir Archibald Sinclair, and
then Chamberlain rose again to say that he felt certain that
he could make a statement of a definite character when the
House met next day. But he still gave no indication of what
was causing the delay.

Three speakers followed him briefly, and then the adjournment was moved.

The Lobbies of the House of Commons were filled with
the buzzing of excited Members, who presently began to
split up and drift away in small parties.

Chamberlain, who had been taken aback by his reception,
called a meeting of the Cabinet immediately, while the
Parliamentary Executive of the Labour Party also met to
consider the situation.

As this now famous scene was being enacted in the House
of Commons, a young couple had had to make a momentous decision. Their banns had already been called, but they
had not intended to marry until later in the month. Shortly
after seven o'clock, the young man, who was working away,
arrived at the home of his future wife unexpectedly.

'I've got until Monday morning,' young Palmer said, 'and
then I don't know what will happen. Do you think we could
get married tomorrow?'

'How can we?' asked his fiancée. 'We haven't got anything
ready.'

'The banns are called,' said the persistent would-be husband, 'you ordered the cake weeks ago, you've got your
dress. If the Vicar would marry us tomorrow, we could get
a few friends together anyhow. If we don't get married now,
God knows when we shall. What do you say? Will you come
and see the Vicar?'

Without further protest, the young woman put on her
coat and went with her young man. Yes, the Vicar would
marry them on Sunday afternoon at two o'clock.

From the Vicarage they hurried to the baker. He had
baked the cake, but it was not decorated, and he could not
possibly ice it in time, since his religious scruples forbade

40

him to work on Sundays, but he would white-ice it. They agreed it would do.

For the next two hours, while the politicians argued and intrigued, they hurried from friend's house to friend's house asking them to be their guests next day, and were happy when a dozen or more replied they would come.

As the future Mr and Mrs Palmer were doing this, at ten o'clock that evening, the Smiths and one or two Estonian friends sat with my wife and me round our German-made radio—the only model on which we could receive the B.B.C. overseas broadcasts intelligibly—and heard the account of what had happened in the House of Commons.

One of the Estonians immediately said, quietly but firmly, 'They will not fight. This is just another kind of Munich!'

We broke up almost at once, for none of us was inclined to talk, and until the small hours I could not sleep, for I knew that if England did not fight, I would have to pack and go home; and if she did, I would still have to go home and fight.

And while I considered how I should organize myself, unknown to me, a ship of the Donaldson Line, the *Athenia*, was slipping down the Clyde from Greenock, with 1,400 passengers and crew aboard, many of them children and 300 of them Americans, on her way to the United States.

And as I struggled with my own personal problems, Winston Churchill was applying himself to his. He was writing again to Chamberlain.

'I have not heard anything from you since our talks on Friday, when I understood that I was to serve as your colleague, and when you told me that this would be announced speedily,' he began.

He went on to say that he had no idea what had happened during that 'agitated' day, though it appeared that events had followed a very different course from what Chamberlain had conveyed to him during their talk. He felt that he must ask the Prime Minister where they stood both privately and publicly before the House met at noon next day. He suggested that if the French were still for delay,

41

then Britain should declare war on her own, and so give the French a lead.

As he wrote, the man to whom he wrote was struggling with just this problem.

2

Act I - Morning

THE RECEPTION which had been given him when he made his statement in the House of Commons had taken Chamberlain completely by surprise, and greatly perturbed him. As soon as the motion for the adjournment was put and accepted, he hurried back to Downing Street and summoned the members of the Cabinet to him.

Though those Ministers who were in closer contact with the ordinary members of the House, and so were able to gauge the general sentiment better than the Prime Minister, could not have been so caught off balance, Chamberlain's reaction did surprise some of them. At the last meeting, many Ministers had believed that it had been agreed that the Prime Minister should announce the sending of the ultimatum at midnight, and they were amazed when he had made no mention of it. Some were now wondering whether they could continue to serve a man who seemed so out of touch, so determined to act according to his own whim, so blind still to the facts that it appeared that he still thought war could be averted.

The time had come for the plainest of plain speaking, and so some of them spoke; and Chamberlain, shaken still by his recent experience in the House, listened and at last accepted the fact that England could not wait for France to make their ultimatum known to the Germans, but would have to act on her own.

With this in view, Chamberlain at once telephoned the French Prime Minister that the House of Commons had made it quite plain that the country would brook no further delay, and that whether the French joined them or not, the British Government would present its ultimatum to Hitler at 8 a.m. to expire at noon. Daladier was sympathetic, but replied that since they had last spoken there had been no change in the French position, and that Chamberlain must do as he thought best.

Chamberlain pleaded with him to get his Government, and especially the military leaders to change their minds, but on receiving no assurance he ended the conversation and returned to the Cabinet room still undecided what to do.

Halifax on the other hand, decided to take some positive action. He sent a coded telegram to the British Ambassador in Berlin, warning him: 'I may have to send you instructions tonight to make an immediate communication to the German Government. Please be ready to act.' This was at ten minutes to midnight. Within the next half hour, it seems, Chamberlain eventually made up his mind, and Halifax sent another telegram to Henderson: 'You should ask for an appointment with the Minister of Foreign Affairs at 9 a.m. on Sunday morning. Instructions will follow.'

While all this had been taking place, a little group of politicians and high-ranking Civil Servants had gathered in the room of Gladwyn Jebb, the private secretary to the Permanent Under-Secretary of State for Foreign Affairs. Jebb's room had been chosen because from its windows the entrance to No. 10 Downing Street could be observed, and the men were anxious to know when the senior Ministers who were attending the Cabinet meeting left.

The men were Hugh Dalton, the Socialist politician, William Strang, the Foreign Office expert on Eastern Europe, Ivane Kirkpatrick, First Secretary at the British Embassy in Berlin, and Jebb. All were anxious to know what was being decided in the house across the street.

At a quarter to one, the watchers saw the door of No. 10 open and a small group of Ministers emerge, and Dalton immediately left the room hoping to buttonhole one of them to discover what decision had been taken. As he went, Kirkpatrick said to him, 'If we rat on the Poles now, we are absolutely sunk, whatever the French do. We shall have no chance against Hitler . . . Even if the French stay out, we shall have the opinion of the world behind us, and we at least have the Poles on our side, with the chance that the United States and others will come in before we are beaten.'

Dalton replied that he hoped if he were asked to decide whether England should fight without the French, his answer would be the same as Kirkpatrick's.

Going down the central staircase of the Foreign Office, Dalton met the Foreign Office legal adviser running up in a great hurry. Dalton asked him how things were going and was told, 'I've got the declaration in the bag now. It is settled now.'

As Dalton reached the side door of the Foreign Office leading into Downing Street, he heard Big Ben striking one o'clock. Lord Halifax was about to enter the Foreign Office, and Dalton told him that he hoped the French had been brought into line, because if not, there would be such an explosion when the House met at noon it might blow up the Government altogether.

'I quite understand,' Halifax replied. 'It has been very difficult, but it will be all right today . . . We may have to go in a few hours before the French, but they will follow all right now.'

Dalton went from the Foreign Office to his flat, from where, at 2 a.m., he telephoned Count Edward Raczynski, the Polish Ambassador in London, and told him the news, adding that he hoped the Ambassador would now be able to get some sleep.

'Yes, if it is true,' replied Raczynski. 'It makes me just a little less unhappy.'

In his office at the Foreign Office, Lord Halifax went to work on the instructions to be telegraphed to the Ambassador in Berlin. By 4 a.m. it was ready, encoded, for dispatch.

At 9 a.m. Sir Nevile was to hand to Ribbentrop a note which, having recalled that a British note of 1st September had called on the Germans to withdraw their troops from Poland immediately, otherwise Great Britain would fulfil her treaty obligations to Poland, informed Hitler, 'Although this communication was made more than twenty-four hours ago, no reply has been received, but German attacks upon

Poland have been continued and intensified. I have accordingly the honour to inform you that, unless not later than 11 a.m., British Summer Time, today 3rd September, satisfactory assurances to the above effect have been given by the German Government and have reached His Majesty's Government in London, a state of war will exist between the two countries as from that hour.'

Henderson received this telegram about four o'clock and immediately telephoned the German Foreign Office in the Wilhelmstrasse. At this time of night, he had some difficulty in finding anyone sufficiently highly placed to make an appointment on behalf of Ribbentrop, who was sleeping and had left orders not to be disturbed on any account.

When the Ambassador insisted that he must see Ribbentrop or his deputy at 9 a.m., he was eventually told that the Foreign Minister would not be available, because of a conference with Hitler timed for that hour, but that he would be received by Dr Paul Schmidt, Hitler's special interpreter, to whom he could hand his communication. With that Henderson had to be content.

While Chamberlain and his Ministers had been meeting and Dalton and his companions had been waiting, the T.S.S. *Athenia* of 13,500 tons, belonging to the Donaldson Atlantic Line, was heading out into the North Atlantic, *en route* for America. She had reached Liverpool from Greenock on the morning of the previous day, picked up more passengers there, and had sailed at 4.30 p.m. By midnight she was off the northern coast of Ireland. As Lord Halifax was putting his final approval to his instructions to the Ambassador in Berlin, she was rolling her way, at a steady fifteen knots past Inishtrahall, the last land she would sight until the coast-line of America came in sight.

While she was battling her way through the heavy Atlantic swell, no one aboard her knew that Oberleutant Fritz Julius Lemp, commander of the U-30, was waiting with his submarine some miles ahead for instructions which, for the last forty-eight hours he was sure would come.

And neither Oberleutant Lemp nor Captain James Cook, master of the *Athenia*, dreamed that before the day was out

46

they would meet, and as a result of the encounter the liner would rest for all time on the ocean bed and sixty-nine women, sixteen children and eight men who had sailed in her would be the first victims of the Second World War.

Many holiday-makers had been caught abroad by the turn of events, and had made arrangements at once for an immediate return to the security of home. Such a one was Douglas Stevens.

'Escaping from Switzerland after a brief holiday,' he says, 'I managed to catch a train from Basle bound, so its placard said, for Calais. This journey, usually a matter of a few hours, was to take fifteen, for on 2nd September, France was rapidly mobilizing.

'It was a most unpleasant and forboding journey, with many changes, and we had to spend at least an hour at the German frontier. Large numbers of refugees crowded in at intervals, filling all the carriages with children and livestock as well as themselves.'

As the train chugged on through the night, wedged in his corner, a feather occasionally floated down from the luggage rack onto his knees. A feather or two he did not mind, but he was in a state of some apprehension that the chickens, tied by the legs and now and again struggling feebly in their petrified fright, might, as a result of this same fright, drop more than feathers.

There was a superstition that such a baptism was an omen of good luck. That might be, he thought, but he would much prefer to reach Calais unmarked. When would this ghastly journey ever end?

Another holiday-maker going in the same direction was Harry Kean, who writes, 'On 18th August, 1939 I went on my motor-cycle in company with my cousin to support the International Six Days' Motor Cycle Trials which were being held at Salzburg. As the tension began to mount, by 25th August most of the British competitors and officials had left for England and home. We were begged by friendly Germans also to leave, and they even provided us with free petrol, which was already rationed.

47

'Being young, I suppose we lacked the experience to read the signs. We even wondered what all the fuss was about, for though Hitler was shouting as usual, he had not yet attacked anyone. So, thinking to let events settle a little, we drove the Norton into Switzerland. When we heard the news that Hitler had marched into Poland, we decided that perhaps the others had been wiser than we had been after all, and we set out across France for home.

'It was an exciting journey, because every few miles along the road, we were stopped by security forces who examined our papers and closely questioned us before allowing us to continue.

'We arrived at the coast late in the afternoon of the 2nd September, and had no difficulty in getting a boat across to Dover. We reached London in the small hours of the Sunday.'

Even though she had got back to London on the Friday, Miss D. Kay, who had been on an Hellenic cruise experienced difficulties which were to increase as the country prepared for war. She had only a cabin trunk with her, and after passing through the customs, she tried to have it sent home by Passenger Luggage in Advance.

'There was an air of feverishness about the station,' she says, 'which was quite unlike the Southern Railway. They refused to take my trunk P.L.A., saying, "We've no idea when you would get it. Take it with you." So there was nothing for it, but the shortage of porters at London and my home station in Cheshire made it one of the worst journeys I have ever made, and I did not get home until long after midnight.'

Maudie Miller, who had just returned from Hollywood, 'where,' she says, 'I was regarded as a fool to want to get back to Britain in the unsettled state of the world,' also experienced many of the early difficulties.

She has recorded in her diary: '31st August: Dental appointment, but find Ferris coping with the Army's teeth, and has to cancel my appointment.

'1st September: Looks definitely like war. Evacuation of London children, first day. Blackout. Very black, like

48

walking among black cotton wool on way home from Ann's flat.

'2nd September: Struggling to get blackout things for windows, in Edgware Road. Evacuation queues at main line stations. Thunderstorm at 11 p.m. Thought war had begun.'

Then there were people who had taken their holiday in the British Isles. As the Cabinet meeting broke up, the Channel Islands packet-boat was butting through the Channel from Southampton heading for Guernsey and Jersey. On board her was Mrs Littlewood, wife of the Vice-Principal of Elizabeth College, the boys' Public School in St Peter Port.

'I had been holidaying in England with my son,' she writes, 'and had arranged to take back to Guernsey with me two sons of a friend who were boarders at Elizabeth College. When the news got so black, I telephoned the friend, who lived in Freshwater in the Isle of Wight, and asked her what she thought about things. I said that I would like to get back to Guernsey, if the balloon were really going to go up. She agreed, and said if I would look after the two boys before term started, she could have them ready for the next day.

'So I got in touch with the Southern Railway, and booked passages for the Saturday night boat. As my friend saw us off she said, "You'll be safe in Guernsey, I'll see you at the end of the war." Little did we know that nine months later we should be packing hurriedly and travelling with suitcases only, leaving our well-stocked homes behind, to begin an exile in England that was to last for five years!'

Then there was Janet Ralston, who had been holidaying with her husband and sister-in-law on Sanday, one of the most northerly of the Orkney Islands. As soon as they had heard the news that Poland had been attacked, they went to Kirkwell, on the Orkney mainland, arriving there in the early afternoon.

'A steamer was due to leave Kirkwell later that afternoon,' says Mrs Ralston, 'to take us to Aberdeen, a ten-hour sail away. But no steamer was waiting at the other berth in the harbour, and we were told that the Government was commandeering every available vessel. There was no word of when a passenger steamer would be available.

'The town was crowded with naval and air force personnel and we found it impossible to get rooms anywhere. We sent telegrams to our families in Glasgow, to tell them not to worry, but found later that they had been delayed by the censorship and we were home almost as soon as they were delivered.

'All night on Friday we hung about the harbour waiting for a ship to arrive. On Saturday morning we had great difficulty in buying food and we were afraid to go far away from the quay in case a ship came in and turned round quickly.

'Late on Saturday afternoon, a steamer arrived from Shetland. It was already crowded with returning holidaymakers and cargo. An air of apprehension hung over everything, yet we were thankful to scramble aboard. At eight o'clock that night we sailed off into the mist and rain.

'All night the rain fell, and many people were sick below decks. We found an alcove on the top deck, and decided to stay outside all night. The fresh air seemed to keep us alert, and none of the three of us was sick. Our sympathies were aroused during the night by the sound every five minutes of what we thought was someone being sick, and presently my husband went to offer help and comfort. In a few minutes he came back laughing. The noise was being made by the rain-water gathering on a tarpaulin over a life-boat, and spilling out when the ship heeled over.

'The voyage took fourteen hours instead of the usual ten, and we landed at Aberdeen early on Sunday morning. By the time we reached home in Glasgow, we had not long to wait to realize what war was going to mean to us all.'

When dawn did come on that September morning, here it was bright and sunny; there the storm clouds had built up and seemed to forbode no good.

In Berlin, as the sleepless British Ambassador bathed and shaved, and changed it was bright and sunny. Despite all his efforts to bring about friendly relations between his country and Nazi Germany, he had failed. Within a short time now, he would be handing over his Government's ultimatum and in this hour of revelation, he knew that only one outcome was possible unless a miracle happened.

Shortly before nine o'clock, he went down to his waiting motor-car and was driven to the Wilhelmstrasse.

Dr Schmidt, who was to receive him on the hour, by a strange quirk of fate had overslept. As he leapt from the taxi which had carried him to the Foreign Office, he saw the Ambassador going up the steps to the main entrance.

Rushing round to a side door, without the Ambassador having seen him, he had just reached Ribbentrop's office as a nearby clock struck the hour and Sir Nevile was announced.

The Ambassador, Dr. Schmidt noted, looked very serious, but he took the interpreter's outstretched hand and shook it. Schmidt asked him to sit down, but Sir Nevile declined, and remained standing in the middle of the room. Without more ado, he read out to Schmidt the British ultimatum in solemn tones.

When he had finished, he handed Schmidt a copy, bowed, and left the room without a word.

At once Schmidt hurried down to the Führer's Chancellery, only a few doors down the Wilhelmstrasse, where Hitler was meeting his ministers and high-ranking Nazi Party officials, several of whom were waiting outside in the ante-room when he arrived.

When he entered, Hitler was sitting at his desk and Ribbentrop was standing by a window. Both looked at him expectantly.

A little distance from the Führer's desk, Schmidt stopped and read a translation of the British ultimatum. For a moment or two, there was complete silence, then Hitler turned to Ribbentrop with a savage look on his face and said, 'What now?'

Quietly Ribbentrop replied, 'I suppose the French will deliver a similar ultimatum within the hour.'

51

Schmidt withdrew to the ante-room, to tell those waiting the news. They also received it in silence.

In a corner of the room, standing by himself, Schmidt saw Goebbels. The Minister for Propaganda and Public Enlightenment looked downcast and self-absorbed.

Drawing Schimdt on one side, Field-Marshal Goering, Chief of the Luftwaffe, said to him, 'If we lose this war, then God have mercy on us.'

At this very moment, at a house in Hamilton in Scotland, the Rutherford family were at breakfast. John Rutherford describes the scene thus: 'My mother was telling us about a dream she had had. It was war, and a ship was burning, and my brother James was in the water.

'As my brother had sailed from Greenock in the *Athenia* twenty-four hours earlier, the rest of us joked and said "more old wives tales".'

But while her children teased her, Mrs Rutherford would not be comforted.

'We'll see,' she said. 'But I hope to God you're right.'

Ribbentrop, who had assured the Führer that Britain would not fight, had been wrong once more when he had said that he expected the French would deliver their ultimatum within the hour.

Not long after Chamberlain had assured the French Prime Minister that the British Government intended to issue their ultimatum at nine o'clock no matter what the French did, Daladier took the initiative and gave instructions that the French Ambassador in Berlin was also to hand over an ultimatum at noon to expire at five o'clock that afternoon. At 10.20 a.m. the French Ambassador in Berlin received his instructions and the French ultimatum.

Now, during the preceding months as the war-clouds had gathered, a Swedish friend of Goering's, a businessman called Berger Dahlerus, had tried to convince the Luftwaffe chief that Britain would not, contrary to Ribbentrop's opinion, stand idly by if Germany carried out any more aggressive acts in Europe.

After some initial difficulty, Dahlerus was able to bring Goering round to his point of view, and having done so had

52

offered himself in the *rôle* of mediator between the two countries.

Dahlerus had several important British connections, who were able to introduce him to Government circles. In the intervening months, he had meetings with highly placed British politicians, including Lord Halifax.

The Swede was a well-meaning man, but he was no diplomat. His role as go-between assumed for him personally an importance it did not possess. The British received and heard him without being impressed.

At eight o'clock on the morning of 3rd September, he heard that the British ultimatum was to be presented an hour later. He hurried to see Goering, according to his own account, and appealed to him to impress upon Hitler the need for a reasonable reply to the British Government, at the same time suggesting that Goering should fly to London before eleven o'clock. Goering said he would put the suggestion to Hitler.

While waitng for the outcome, Dahlerus, at 10.15 a.m. telephoned the British Foreign Office on his own initiative, to say that a reasonable reply was on the way. At ten-fifty— ten minutes before the ultimatum expired—he telephoned again, announcing that Hitler had agreed to Goering's flying immediately to London.

In unequivocal terms, Lord Halifax told Dahlerus that it was quite impossible for such a thing to happen at this late hour.

While these events were taking place, young Palmer, who had persuaded his fiancée and his Vicar that they must be married that day, was up early and making a round of the back doors of shops to try to find some decorations for the wedding cake which the baker would only white-ice. On his return to his future father-in-law's house, having been partially successful, he was met with the news that the B.B.C. had just announced that the Prime Minister was going to talk to the nation at a quarter past eleven.

'It can mean only one of two things,' said his fiancée's father. 'Peace or war, and I reckon it will be war. I'm going to make a dug-out in the garden, and I'll be grateful for any help I can get.'

Taking the hint, young Palmer fetched a spade, and throughout the morning of his wedding day he dug a hole in his fiancée's lawn.

While young Palmer was digging, Duff Cooper was at a meeting of the small parliamentary group of Conservatives who were opposed to Chamberlain's policies, in the house of Ronald Tree in Queen Anne's Gate.

When the House had risen on the previous evening, Duff Cooper had fetched his wife, Lady Diana, from their house in Chapel Street, and they had gone to the Savoy Grill for supper. Duff Cooper has recorded that he did not feel hungry, 'but dealt successfully with a cold grouse.' There they had been joined by Ronald Tree and James Thomas, who were feeling, as he was, angry and depressed by what had happened in the House.

About half past ten, he went to Winston Churchill's flat where Anthony Eden, Robert Boothby, Brendon Bracken and Duncan Sandys were already deep in a heated argument. Churchill himself considered that Chamberlain had treated him very badly because though he had agreed to join the Government the previous evening, the Prime Minister had ignored him throughout the entire day. He had wanted to speak in the House that evening, but considering himself as good as in the Government, he had refrained.

As Duff Cooper entered, Boothby was saying that Chamberlain had forfeited the trust of the Conservative Party forever, and he was sure that if Churchill wished he had it in his power to break him in the House on Sunday and take his place. Further more, he was of the opinion that Churchill should refuse to serve under Chamberlain, for if he did he would save him.

They argued about this for several hours, and then news arrived that the ultimatum was to be delivered at 9 a.m. and that unless it were accepted, the Prime Minister would announce that we were at war. This changed the situation, and the anger cooled. It was at this point that Churchill decided to send his letter to the Prime Minister, to which previous reference has been made.

Now the rebels were meeting briefly to decide on their

course of action, should action be called for. They were still there when the ultimatum expired.

When Big Ben boomed out eleven o'clock, no reply had come from Berlin.

At eleven-fifteen the Prime Minister's voice was heard from every loud-speaker in the country. No one who heard that brief broadcast announcing that England was at war with Germany could have failed to be moved by the sadness in the voice of the man who in this moment saw all he had worked for over the past year and more, smashed into smithereens at his feet. Even his critics in his own Party, Duff Cooper has recorded, 'All thought he did it very well.'

I heard him speak in Madame Torvand-Tellmann's flat in Tallinn, where the time was quarter past twelve. During the morning the friends who had been with us the previous evening returned. I think they did not wish us to be alone, which was typical of their sympathy and generosity.

We listened in silence, and I saw my wife draw to her our small son who was playing at our feet, take him on her knee and hold him tightly, while noiseless tears coursed down her cheeks. I knew exactly what her thoughts were; I knew what her feelings were; but from my man's point of view, I could not but be glad that though the future might bring difficulty, even tragedy, into our lives, at least it would bring freedom from the fear of tyrants for our son and his sister.

I switched off the radio as soon as the Prime Minister had finished speaking, and wished we were alone. Perhaps our friends sensed what I was thinking, for they all rose, shook us warmly by the hand and said they would return in the evening.

As one young man took my hand, he smiled sadly and said, 'We knew England would fight. Now we can breathe again.'

Within a year he had died at the hands of a Russian firing squad.

One of Madame Torvand-Tellmann's daughters had returned from the country the evening before with her husband, a brilliant young Austrian concert pianist, called Hans Hoepfel, both had tried to cheer us up, telling us that there

55

would be no war, and Hoepfel had sat down at the piano and played several of the stirring polonaises of Chopin. Only an hour before, Madame Hoepfel had come upon me in the kitchen and had said, 'Cheer up, Härra, it will all be over in a week or two.'

When we had woken that morning I had told my wife that if war came I wanted to go home immediately, and I hoped she would agree.

'You must make the decisions,' she had said, quietly.

Having seen our guests to the door, I went into the room where the telephone was, to telephone the British Legation to tell the Chargé d'Affaires that I was leaving as soon as possible. Hans Hoepfel was there, and to my great surprise, he jumped up from his chair and rushed from the room without a word, and a scared look in his eyes.

Not knowing quite how to take it, I shrugged my shoulders and dialled the Legation number. I asked the duty clerk to put me through to Wilfred Gallienne, a Guernseyman, who represented His Majesty in Estonia as Consul and Chargé d'Affaires.

When Gallienne said, 'Yes, Seth?' I told him what I intended to do.

'I'm afraid you can't,' he said sternly.

'Oh, why not?' I asked.

'The Foreign Office have given instructions that all British Nationals living here are to remain where they are until they are told what to do.'

'I can understand people being employed by the Government being told what to do, and having to comply,' I answered. 'But I am not employed by the British Government, nor the British Council nor a British firm, so I do not think the Foreign Office can tell me what to do. I repeat, I am taking my family home at once.'

'You do so at your own risk, then,' Gallienne snapped, and rang off.

I could not understand this attitude of the Foreign Office. Surely, I thought, it would be better to get all Englishmen who were not in essential posts home before it was too late, for as I appreciated the situation, this part of the world would be cut off from easy access with England, was even now so cut off. I believed that as the war got into swing, both air and sea passages across the North Sea from Norway would be fraught with risks from U-boat and aircraft. If such a journey were to be made with the best chances of success, now was the time for it.

So we were the only English family to leave Estonia then, and as things turned out, I have always been glad that I made my decision, for when the Germans attacked Russia, the British colony in Estonia were evacuated via Moscow, the Trans-Siberian Railway and Vladivostok to Australia, from where, if they had their own resources, they had to make their own way home, and if they had not, they had to stay.

As I left the room, in the passage outside, I met Madame Hoepfel who was waiting for me.

'We are going back to the country until you have gone,' she said.

'But why on earth——?' I began.

'Don't you understand that Hans and I and you and your family, we are enemies now?' she said. 'If someone ever told the Legation here (meaning the German Legation) that we had stayed in the same house as you we should be in very great trouble.'

'But we shall be gone by Tuesday at the latest,' I tried to assure her. But it was no good. They had already thrown some clothes into a bag, and five minutes later were gone.

Back in Scotland a small boy of fourteen was sitting on the seat in the bay-window of his parent's living-room overlooking the River Clyde as the radio behind him brought the Prime Minister's sad voice into the room. What came out of the loudspeaker made no impact on him, for his attention was fixed on a paddle steamer making its way up the river.

Suddenly the black, lowering clouds which had been piling up during the last couple of hours, parted for a second's fraction and emitted a vivid fork of lightning. Fascinated, the boy watched the lightning stripe downwards and saw it lick the steamer which gave a violent shudder.

'Young though I was,' Lieutenant-Commander A. G. Arnot

57

says twenty-three years later, 'I was impressed by this sign of ill-omen. For family reasons, this manifestation was made rather more impressive as, when we were children, our father used to tell my sister and me that, should we get frightened in a thunder storm, we should remember that thunder was only God rolling barrels about in Heaven and lightning was when he clapped his hands.'

Another boy, a couple of years older than young Arnot, had already had a strange experience. Major D. G. Miles, R.A., the boy, has described his outstanding memory of this day.

'I was sixteen years old at the time,' he has written, 'and lived with my family in a small village in Wiltshire. My father was in the Army, serving at H.Q. Southern Command at Salisbury. He was on duty at his office all night on the Saturday night, and did not return home until Sunday evening.

'During the night there was a very heavy thunderstorm, which woke us all. Early on Sunday morning a villager called at our house and told my mother that a strange woman appeared to have been sleeping on a seat by the 1914-1918 War Memorial, just by our garden. My mother went out and found the woman there, sitting on the seat wet through.

'She took her in and gave her breakfast, and soon realized that she was a lunatic. I remember coming down to breakfast, unaware of what had been going on, to be confronted by this strange unkempt woman hungrily devouring chipolatas and talking gibberish.

'Meanwhile my mother had rung up the Salisbury Asylum and discovered that the woman had escaped from there the previous afternoon. They were delighted to hear of her whereabouts and promised to send someone to collect her immediately. After breakfast the woman had a bath while we waited.

'By this time our daily help, Mrs Hazard, had heard about the woman and had come round to see if she could help my mother.

'The people from the asylum arrived about eleven o'clock, and when they had gone we all went into the drawing-room

58

and listened to Mr Chamberlain's speech on the wireless. I well remember Mrs Hazard bursting into tears when the Prime Minister said "a state of war exists".

'I believe it was just a little after this that the local policeman came round and said that we should put black paint on the reflectors of our car head-lamps. This we did, thereby incurring my father's wrath when we went to collect him from his office that evening.'

The fact that we were at war reacted on people, it seems, according to their temperament. Mrs E. L. Coggan, who now lives in Northern Transvaal, writes, 'My husband and I did the usual skimpy Sunday morning chores and finished about five minutes before Mr Neville Chamberlain was due to speak to the world.

'My husband settled himself in an easy chair, but I was restless, and knelt on the settee where I could look out of the window. We were on the third floor, level with the tree tops, whose branches were showing as the leaves had just started to fall.

'Mr Chamberlain started to speak and while I listened with dread, the thought ran through my mind over and over, "It cannot be! We CANNOT have another war. Everyone MUST know that war is futile and can get no one anywhere worthwhile. The other war was too recent. Surely no one wants another war. I cannot believe it. But it is happening. How can mankind be so stupid?"

'All the while, a man in the drive below was polishing his car, as if nothing unusual was going on. Rub, rub, rub, now round the front again, unfasten the doors and rub their insides. Now the windows. Who is this man who can calmly clean his car just as he has done every Sunday morning for years? Why doesn't someone yell at him that the whole world is going mad again? How can he just go on all along rubbing and rubbing a car which he may never use again?'

On the other hand, Captain E. G. M. Roe, pointing out that 3rd September was already a multi-anniversary—the Battle of Worcester was fought on this day in 1651, Oliver Cromwell died on it in 1658, and Captain Roe's uncle was born on it—goes on:

'I was at home, having just returned from camp, and was eating a late breakfast of bacon and fried bread. I was alone, the rest of the family having gone to church, but I had the radio and the cat for company.

'As I listened to the sepulchral tones of Mr Neville Chamberlain, then Prime Minister, I realized things had gone from bad to worse in my absence, and when he finished the ominous wail of the air-raid sirens began, I put down my knife and fork and went over to the window, I could see the balloons all going up into the sky like lifts, until hundreds of these silver sausages floated over London.

'This is it, I told the cat, and realizing that I could do nothing about it, we both sat down to breakfast again, I to my bacon, he to his rinds. We were soon interrupted by a gentle but persistent and agitated knocking at the front door. I had to put down my knife and fork again.

'A very distressed lady, livid of countenance and perspiring profusely, stood at the door.

' "Oh," she panted, "May I use your telephone, please?"

' "Certainly," I said, "come in." I led the way into the room where I had been breakfasting and where the telephone was. "There you are," I said. "Help yourself!"

'She tried to dial, but her fingers fluttered so much that she could not manage it, so I got the number for her and then resumed my breakfast.

'I paid no attention to her conversation, but when she had finished she explained that her children were at their aunt's without their gas-masks, and she wanted to ensure they stayed there until the raid was over. "And you," she said suddenly. "How can you sit there calmly eating eggs and bacon at a time like this?"

' "Madam," I said. "What am I supposed to do? Do you expect me to rush out and repel German bombers with a knife and fork?"

'The shock of this highly reasonable suggestion had the desired effect of bringing her down to earth, but she was still too confused to pay for the telephone call when she left.'

Then there was the young poet Michael Marais, who was a sensitive boy of seventeen at the time, who put his thoughts and reactions into the following poem which he has very kindly allowed me to quote.

SEPTEMBER 3RD, 1939

Sunday morning I was shaving
the bathroom door ajar
and at seventeen having
to take particular care
(pimples, a cut-throat razor) then
carried from downstairs
the voice of that inadequate old man
calling up latent fears.

Caught me that sudden sickly mortal feeling
a Jesus-this-is-it
awareness, first of how many following
before I'd done with it?
Initiate in the bathroom, fear thrilling
with death-thoughts, live, Life-size,
realities crowded shrilling
to oust child fantasies.

Could we have but foreknown
thrills' overspilling,
men's ingenuity man's inhumanity has shown
to deal with killing
—but seen what expertise was soon begetting
what careful skills to expedite bloodletting!

In his accompanying letter he said, 'Though the piece suffers from (amongst other things) lack of development it is accurate as personal reminiscence and probably has a pretty general application as regards my age-group. I was still at school, a dayboy at a local minor public school. Like many of my contemporaries, I'd seen the relevance of the Spanish War, been ashamed of Britain's attitude, dismayed by the expressed isolationism of our parents.

61

'Later I joined the R.A.F.V.R. and was a pilot, did forty-odd operations in the Middle East with 38 Squadron on night torpedo and bombing strikes against shipping, low-level attacks mainly on coastal targets and anti-submarine patrols . . .

'When I think about that Sunday morning in the bathroom I still feel sick; it's absolutely convincing; the memory gives me an emotional jolt much more clearly defined than any relating to subsequent experiences.

'I hope we're not as acquiescent as were our parents. Perhaps we're not quite so tolerant of the inadequate old men. At any rate, today I am a unilateralist and like to encourage in the young any signs of intelligent disrespect for paternalistic Authority and Government.'

John Howes, an Australian living in Caulfield, Victoria, had very different emotions.

'My first thought,' he has written, 'was that gallant Britain had once again declared war to defend our democratic way of life, while powerful America, as usual, was to wait until forced into the war for freedom at a later date.

'My second thought was for the gallant British people whom I knew would receive a far worse bombing than the Zeppelin raids, some of which I witnessed as a patient in hospital in England in 1916-1918. I thought again of the heroism displayed by the English people during the air-raids of World War I, a heroism only equalled by the wonderful hospitality and kindness they extended to me, as wounded Australian, sharing even their meagre rations with me until I discovered they were doing so.

'I remember a beloved King and Queen whose hospitality I enjoyed at Windsor Castle, when they received me as a representative of Australia's wounded.

'My next thought was for my son, who, like me, would fight in his teenage at Tobruk and El Alamein. (Later, when it was all over, I was proud of his answer when I asked him what Tobruk and Alamein were like, and he said, "Why talk about them when there was London and Coventry?")

'Now I have other thoughts, but let them be. The one thing that remains in my mind, and will do so until journey's end, is gratitude to the English people for their kindness, admiration of their heroism, and always the prayer that my beloved England will never be bombed again.'

Perhaps the Monarch summed up the feelings of many of those who carried the responsibility of leading the nation, when he wrote in his diary that night, 'As eleven o'clock struck on this fateful morning, I had a certain feeling of relief that those ten anxious days of negotiations with Germany over Poland, which at moments looked favourable, with Mussolini working for peace, were over . . .

'At the outbreak of war at midnight on 4th/5th August, 1914, I was a midshipman, keeping the middle watch on the bridge of H.M.S. *Collingwood* at sea somewhere in the North Sea. I was eighteen years of age. In the Grand Fleet everyone was pleased that it had come at last. We had been trained in the belief that war between Germany and this country had to come one day, and when it did come we thought we were well prepared for it. We were not prepared for what we found a modern war really was, and those of us who had been through the Great War never wanted another.

'Today we are at war again, and I am no longer a midshipman in the Royal Navy. For the last year, ever since the Munich agreement, Germany, or rather its leaders, have caused us incessant worry in crises of different magnitudes . . . We knew the Polish question would be the next on the list of Hitler's bloodless victories. The whole country knew it and had been preparing for it by making arms and aeroplanes and all the engines of war in record time to withstand the next real crisis.

'So today, when the crisis is over and the result of the breakdown of negotiations is war, the country is calm, firm and united behind its leaders, resolved to fight until liberty and justice are once again safe in the world . . .'

From the many reminiscences which have been sent to me, it is clear that even when children were intellectually mature to understand that war can be horrible, they were puzzled often by the grown-up reactions to the first news. For example, Mrs Patricia Shepherd, who was thirteen, went with her mother, her brother of eighteen, and her sisters of sixteen and ten, to Church, as was the family custom.

'But in place of the sermon,' she writes, 'we had the announcement of war from the Vicar, who had just been informed of the Prime Minister's broadcast.

'Everyone, I remember, looked worried and tearful. I could not understand their worry. If we had beaten the Germans before, we could certainly do so again, I reasoned.

'However, it was to change my pattern of life completely. My parents decided, after much heart-searching, to send me and my two sisters to an aunt and uncle in South Africa, where we stayed for the duration of the war. I was to meet the man who later became my husband; my son was born in South Africa; I was widowed in South Africa. I returned again to England and later married again someone I had known as a child . . . My son is now fourteen and appears to be just as confident about winning World War III if it comes as I was at thirteen about winning World War II.'

Peter Stucley was thirty, and was working with the B.B.C. in Bristol, and was in the Bush Hotel at Farnham, when the Prime Minister spoke. In his diary that night he recorded: 'We listened in the hotel lounge. Everyone very quiet and sad. One couple afterwards in tears saying they wished they had lived better lives. One can't help feeling a relief, however, ghastly things to come may be, that it has actually begun, and though war is always terrible and disgraceful, the reason for starting this one does seem justifiable.

'It appears to us as aggression and unforgivable arrogance by the Germans. Everyone was ready to negotiate except the Germans, who declared force must be met by force. It seems impossible to believe we are at war and must be prepared to die. Mother wonderfully courageous all the time —and this is the second time for her. I left after lunch and drove back to Huntstrete and John. I noticed, as I drove past Upavon, dozens of bombers laid out on the airfield all ready to leave.'

Naturally it was the parents of children old enough to be involved who felt it most.

In the little church of St Mary Magdalene, in the small

Norfolk village, an old lady of seventy-two sat straight-backed in her pew. Her son and daughter-in-law had been holidaying with her, but as the international situation had grown increasingly critical, the son had decided to return to London, and his Queen had felt it her duty to be with him.

So Queen Mary was alone in the royal pew.

The Rector, Mr Fuller, had brought his wireless into the church and set it up in the nave, and at quarter past eleven, he paused in the service to hear the Prime Minister's announcement.

That evening Queen Mary noted in her diary: 'Everyone was silent but it was a tense moment and one could only hope and pray.'

In this she was joined by all the mothers of England.

'When I heard the Prime Minister say we were at war,' says Mrs. M. Walker, 'I felt so sad. It was a day like any other Sunday, but London was very subdued. Most of the children had been evacuated, including my own two boys, who were still at school. I hoped and prayed that it would all be over before they would be called up. But it wasn't! My eldest boy joined the Navy and was killed.'

Queen Mary also lost a son.

Mrs V. A. Deadman was in her garden at eleven-fifteen hanging nappies on a line. As she did so a neighbour called over the hedge, "We're at war. I've just heard it on the wireless!"

Mrs Deadman says, 'I just looked at the line of washing, speechless. Then presently I heard my two-year-old son—now in the R.A.F.—saying, "What's the matter, Mummy?"

'I ran to him and picked him up. "Nothing, dear," I said. "Everything is all right." Whatever happened, I had to protect my children.'

Several clergymen had, like Mr Fuller at Sandringham, taken their wireless sets to church. In most cases, the solemnity which Queen Mary noted was present, but in one Berkshire church it was not so marked.

A member of the congregation had brought his portable wireless and set it up in the chancel steps. The Vicar had decided not to begin the service until after the announcement, and a few minutes before eleven-fifteen, he switched on the set to see that it was properly tuned in. Immediately a woman's voice filled the church. 'Take an onion, peel it . . .' she said, before she was hastily switched off.

The B.B.C. came in for much criticism during the early days of the War, criticism which since has not been modified much. At the time it was based on ignorance of the situation which faced the Corporation, and the fact that the broadcasting services were not only maintained at all, but were actually extended insofar as actual 'time on the air' was concerned, makes the criticism all the more unhappy.

Before the war, broadcasting had been operated on a regional basis, with a central programme known as the National. The regions were responsible for the great percentage of their output, and the regional network put out National programmes when these programmes were of major importance. The National station was also responsible for the general news bulletins.

In their consideration of the role which the B.B.C. would be called upon to play if war ever did break out, the Governors and the Director-General had decided that their problems would be much simplified if the regional organization were replaced by one national service, to be called the Home Service. Like a great many commercial firms, they had also planned that except for the news services, all the other departments of the Corporation should be evacuated to the country, where emergency transmitters were also secretly prepared.

As soon as the crisis showed signs of developing into war, on 1st September it was decided that the evacuation plan should be put into operation the following day. The uprooting of whole departments from London to the 'country' was a task, of which, I suggest, the true magnitude can be appreciated only by those responsible and by those who took part.

Until the operation was completed, it was physically impossible for a variety of programmes to go out over the air. The situation required, however, that there should be continuous broadcasting so that people would keep their sets tuned in and so hear emergency announcements which had to be made.

The only feasible solution was that which the B.B.C. adopted; news bulletins, Government announcements and suitable talks interlarded with programmes of gramophone music and Sandy Macphearson at the cinema organ. It was the seemingly endless stream of gramophone records which provoked most of the criticism.

In these days, and for the last twenty years and more, we have become so accustomed to being able to switch on our sets at 6.30 a.m. to be entertained at that hour by the B.B.C., that it has been forgotten that up to 2nd September, 1939, daily broadcasting had not begun until 10 a.m.

The Home Service had come into operation at about 5.15 p.m. on the 1st September, and it had been laid down that every two hours throughout the night a news and announcement bulletin should be broadcast. This arrangement was discontinued after a short time when it was discovered that there was insufficient new material coming in during the night to make these broadcasts worthwhile. But it was decided that in future broadcasting should begin daily at 6 a.m., and continue uninterrupted until midnight.

By Sunday, the Home Service was beginning to get into its stride. The broadcast service arranged for the National programme to come from Croydon Parish Church, came on the air at nine twenty-five. The two hymns sung at that service, though chosen weeks before, could not have been more appropriate. They were *O for a faith which will not shrink* and *God is working His purpose out*.

Whoever was responsible for making-up the programmes of records was obviously intent to stress that though we were at war, we must not forget that love is really the main motive force of man's existence. The programme broadcast at midday consisted of five pieces, of which three were *The Indian Love Song*, Greig's *Norwegian Bridal Procession* and *Un Sonnet d'Amour*.

In the middle of the afternoon listeners were to be diverted by a programme called *Proverbs—a Parlour Game for Listeners* conducted by Mr Frederick Grisewood. This was

67

really a forerunner of all such radio games like Twenty Questions and What's My Line.

Proverbs was followed at five o'clock by a talk by Dom Bernard Clements, the famous Vicar of All Saints, Margaret Street. His theme could scarcely have been more appropriate—*What happens when I die?*

But the main broadcast of the day was undoubtedly the Prime Minister's. Most clergymen who had not taken radios into church, made arrangements to be informed immediately of what Mr Chamberlain had said, and at once told their congregations. Some, like the Reverend H. J. A. Rushbridger, prepared two sermons—one if the news was peace, one if it was war.

Miss S. M. Isaacson heard that it was war in St Mary Abbot's church. She says, 'It was while walking back from my office in Westminster that I saw at Hyde Park Corner a *Daily Express* placard with five words in gigantic lettering THERE WILL BE NO WAR. That was about 3 p.m. on the Saturday. I was in St. Mary Abbot's church at 11 a.m. next morning and heard Mr Chamberlain's words read from the pulpit, followed almost immediately by the deafening siren which was operated from the police station adjoining the church.

'I think most of us felt that London was about to be obliterated and did not quite know what to do, but an old lady near me said quietly, "Don't you think the church is the best place to be until the All Clear?" The combination of news, siren and the old lady's calm have made that Sunday unforgettable for me.'

Mrs Joan Cattley was on holiday with two children, one her own, the other a Jewish refugee from Germany, near Lough Corrib in Western Ireland.

She writes: 'Our hostess was organist at the parish church. She dropped us at an hotel to hear the Prime Minister's speech on the wireless while she went to prepare for the service. After the P.M's opening sentences I fled down the street to the church to tell her the news, shouting as I went, "England is at war! England is at war!" The local peasantry, on their way to Mass, merely stared. It was no concern of theirs—why this agitation and excitement? they seemed to be saying.'

The Reverend C. D. Stewart Robinson was Vicar at South Nutfield, in Surrey.

'The morning service was to be at 11 a.m.,' he says. 'At ten-thirty my church-warden came to me minus coat and said he was off to Wales with his wife as there was going to be war and that the Prime Minister was to speak over the radio at 11 a.m.

'I called the Verger and my sister-in-law, and told them to listen, and at whatever part of the service, the Verger was to bring me a written notice.

'The service started, and just before the Second Lesson the Verger came and handed me the notice which I read out. One or two air-raid wardens left at once for duty. I had only been in the pulpit a few moments when the Verger handed me another notice, "Air-raid warning in operation."

'I advised the congregation and said that I would close the service as we did not know what to expect. My wife hurried to the Vicarage and set about making a gas-proof room. I cancelled Sunday School as I was not taking any risks with children under one roof. Then we heard that the siren had sounded because of an unidentified aircraft, and so the phoney war started.'

Though it had been expected for days, when the news came there was scarcely a soul who was not shocked by it to a greater or lesser degree.

Before the war, Mrs Louise Derrick had a little ladies' hair-dressing business, and on Sunday morning she was 'doing a perm for a customer who was getting married next day.'

'I was half-way through when we heard on the radio that war had been declared,' she says. 'We both burst into tears, I wondering what would happen to my baby boy, for whom I had waited eight years; she because all her plans for a beautiful white wedding seemed to have been smashed.'

Mrs Mary Frankland was a young nurse in a maternity hospital. She was sitting on a patient's bed rolling bandages as she listened to the radio.

'I will never forget,' she says, 'the faces of those young mothers who had just had or were about to have their babies. They all knew that their husbands would have to go to war, and that they would not be able to share the joy of bringing up their babies together.'

G. A. Shirer was taking his dog for a walk, and shortly after eleven-fifteen he was overtaken by a child on a tricycle, who told him the news.

'We both looked up at the sky. I was undecided whether to continue or go back. Such was the air-raid mentality that had been instilled into us and exaggerated by the black-out of the two previous days. But I went on, and called on the Ps. She said, "What do we do next?" "Get the dinner!" he said, and I decided that that was the only attitude to take.'

In his diary that night, Hubert Leslie described his reactions thus: 'Those of the congregation who came to church this morning whispered in my ear (I was ushering) that war had been declared . . . Although it was what we were all expecting, and in the hope of exterminating the Nazi terror, half-hoping for, it made me feel quite sick for a few minutes. I cannot and dare not attempt to analyse my feelings; I suppose they were much like what everyone else was feeling, a sort of numbness of mind, as if the end of the world had suddenly come. However, this soon wore off, and I was able to think normally again, and to see that it was just this very thing that we had been arming for for the last few years, we and France and all Europe; and, that from a horribly human point of view, it was inevitable.

'With this ghastly news in mind, it was difficult to keep one's thoughts on the service; and yet the words of the readings were most beautifully chosen, including the 91st Psalm.

'One poor lady, who told me that she had been fitting gas-masks all day, said that all her dear ones were "in it," and she was here all alone, trying to do her bit. She was terribly wrought up, and asked me, "How must we see this?" I could not talk to her, being on duty, but for myself it seemed to me that the quotation from the (Christian Science) textbook, (page 115) which came in this week's lesson, were very apt.

' "Scientific Translation of Mortal Mind, First Degree: Depravity, evil beliefs, passions and appetites, fear, depraved will, self-justification, pride, envy, deceit, hatred, revenge, sin, sickness, disease, death."

'And as those items were read out I could not help seeing how accurately they tally with the Nazi creed—Evil beliefs, the worship of the Swastika and Personality; Passions, the brutality against all who differ from them; Fear, which is in the heart of every cruel bully; Depraved will, or, as Chamberlain put it, "senseless Ambition"; Self-justification, those endless reiterations of "the rightness of everything Hitler does"; Pride, the megalomania with which the Nazis are eaten up; Envy, of every other people's possessions and land and wealth; Deceit, as exemplified in all their diplomacy; Hatred, like their ferocious pogroms against the Jews and their overflowing concentration camps; Revenge on all who oppose them.

'It is not the Germans, it isn't even Hitler that we are warring against; it is this bloody denial of God in every phase of the Nazi creed, which is enslaving not only Germany but all others weaker than themselves; it is this damnable doctrine which has simply got to be rooted out if men are ever again to be able to live in peace.

'During the service there was a "trial alarm", which was a bit stupid, for who, in church, could know but that it wasn't a real scare. One doctor came with his car to fetch his wife home, much against her will, poor dear, for I feel that she felt she ought to be in church whatever was happening outside.

'A young woman came, carrying a gas-mask, to call for a child in the Sunday School and to take her home. Apart from these interruptions, the service was a great help to all of us; and the church was very full, too.

'Our crêche is going strong and enjoying life in spite of the squash in the house and the alarums and excursions of the news bulletins. (We had two little girls and a small boy billeted on us.) Happily they cannot possibly realize what all the fuss is about, and they haven't even asked awkward questions. Poor Richard H. aged six, was left here by his

71

mother and he hasn't yet sorted out who's who in this jumbled household. There are seven people he has never set eyes on before, so it is understandable that he should think that Peter (our youngest son) is my elder brother and that Molly D. is my mother.

'I made out for each member of the household a sheet of paper with their name on it, and a map of this address, with our name on it and our phone number; the whole thing, only a half-sheet of note-paper, with a map printed on it in an envelope, with a string stapled to one corner. Each of the kids has to have it tied to them, and the rest of us just wear them in some pocket or other, so that if we did get knocked out at any time, the good Samaritans who find us will know where to return us; or if the kids get separated in a pannicky crowd they can show the map to someone and get brought home safely.

'My black-out lamp-shades are going well; twelve already sold, and twelve more on order for tomorrow. I'm thinking of trying to get the Eagle Press to punch me out some discs for the job, instead of having to use cheese-boxes every time. We've enough cheese to start a Cut Price Shop.

'I'm still waiting for a customer to come and complain that when his patent "H.L. Black-out Lamp-shade" has been in use for some time there rises an all pervading odour of toasted cheese, for the boxes I use must be fairly impregnated with cheese, and the heat of the lamp might start cooking it!'

(Mr Leslie did get some cardboard discs for the job, and a hundred or more of his shades before they were massed produced and in the shops. He was a Silhouettist, and so had a stock of black paper with which to make the shades.)

There is much evidence to show that many people had undoubtedly been impressed by the official warnings to expect immediate German air attacks of great violence, some to such an extent that they were overcome by their fears.

Mrs O. M. Calver was at her home in Petts Wood, alone with her two-year-old baby and expecting another. The garden ran down to a railway cutting which often held the morning mist until the sun cleared it away.

Shortly after eleven-fifteen there was a violent banging on her front door, and when she opened it, she was confronted by an elderly lady complete with hymn-book who was on the verge of hysterics.

'Let me in! Let me in!' she shouted. 'They're coming! They're coming!'

'Who are coming?' Mrs Calver asked, and was told, "The Germans! You can see the gas all the way along the railway line!"

Mrs Calver let her in, and explained quietly that what she thought was gas was mist. Presently her guest quietened and became rational.

'Can I do anything to help you?' she asked.

'Yes.' Mrs Calver told her. 'Peel the potatoes!'

Others, realizing what the future would hold, thought only of seizing a few moments peace.

J. Fern-Ellis was in North Wales. 'After listening to Chamberlain we decided to get into the car and go into the peace and quiet of Snowdonia. It was all very grey and still . . . and we wondered when we would next take a motor ride into these peaceful hills and valleys. But at least we had these quiet moments to remember, whatever happened.'

Whoever was responsible for deciding to test the air-raid sirens immediately after the Prime Minister had spoken, and to do so without giving a warning that it was a test, was certainly a man of little imagination.

The reactions to the wailing were as varied as to the news of war.

Mrs D. P. Anderson was at home in Brighton. 'I was shaken by the news, particularly as the only person in the house was a simple maid who did not appreciate what was happening, and the old man working in the garden was deaf and dumb.

'Then the warning went. Knowing I must keep calm my first thought was to tell the maid to make a cup of tea and to tell Dummy, as we called the gardner, to come into the house out of danger. I watched from the windows to see how she would accomplish this.

'The pantomime was one I shall never forget. After much

73

gesticulating from the girl, Dummy seemed to understand. Then he looked up at the sky with withering contempt, spat scornfully, grabbed the mower and went on with his work. He steadied my nerves better than any cup of tea.'

Mrs Doris Croft decided to ignore the warning and went into the kitchen to continue preparing the midday meal. As she started using an egg-beater, her father called to her from the sitting-room, 'Hark! The beggars haven't lost any time starting their wicked tricks.' He had thought the noise of the egg-beater was the rattle-warning announcing a gas-attack.

Mrs M. I. Cottrell's husband was a fully trained A.R.P. Warden and as the siren went, says his wife, he exclaimed, 'We're for it now! This is the end!', and decided that all his training must be put into full operation at once, so began rushing round issuing orders.

'He decided our kitchen should be our refuge, and my elderly mother and her friend were hurried in. All available blankets were taken off the beds, some being nailed to the top of the doors and windows in case of gas attacks. The oven cloth was stuffed up the boiler chimney. I was given rolls of sticky tape which I hastily stuck over the cracks in the windows and back door, meanwhile filling the sink with water in case of fire.

'My mother sat on one kitchen chair with her canary in its cage on one knee and a bottle of whisky on the other, in case of emergency. Her friend was very nearly fainting with the heat and fright.

'My husband then decided he must look after the rest of the street, and seeing an unconcerned couple about to go for a Sunday drive in their car, yelled at the top of his voice, "Take cover, take cover!"'

'Fortunately the All Clear soon sounded and we emerged shaken but safe. The only ill-effects of the preparations were that next day we were nearly choked by smoke when we lit the boiler, having forgotten the oven cloth was still in the chimney.'

The public-minded citizens who had offered themselves for A.R.P. duties and had attended instruction had had impressed upon them the then official view that Hitler

74

would launch an all-out air attack in the first hours of the war. Very properly they took their duties and their training seriously, but this often led them into behaviour which in retrospect seems exaggerated.

On the other hand, there appears to have been a partial failure in communication between the authorities and the public; or the public, in their refusal to believe that there could be war, had not listened with full attention; or perhaps it was a combination of both.

This first Alert produced much evidence of misunderstanding or total ignorance of what should be done in an emergency; though some of the variations in behaviour arose from the normal variations between individuals in temperament.

Thus Mrs Ringer reports that as the warning sounded, 'Almost everybody in the street where we lived came to their doors to see what was happening,' while Mrs Watts, who was waiting in the bus station at Sheerness for a Maidstone bus, says, 'I never before saw a bus empty so quickly or the streets so deserted.'

William Mallory was a part-time warden. He says: 'Orders to wardens were that on an alarm sounding, all Civil Defence people on street duty were to don gas-clothing. So out I went swathed to the eyes in protective clothing.

'When I had managed to persuade all the householders on my beat to stop gazing into the sky from their front gardens and get indoors, I met a middle-aged man pushing a small child in a go-cart along the street.

'He and I were the only human beings in sight. I said, "Don't you know there's an alert? Get yourself and the child under cover! Any of these houses will take you in." He replied, "Who the hell are you? Mind your own business!"

'At that moment the All Clear sounded. I have sometimes wondered what I would have done if it hadn't, but I think my conviction that we would win the war, dated from that moment.'

On the other hand, Mrs A. H. Ozanne recalls, 'I was staying in Hove and on the Sunday morning, I was on the pier

75

at Brighton I was surprised when men came and closed the kiosks and turned everyone off. Leaving the pier, I was strolling back along the front to my hotel, when I suddenly realized I was quite alone. Not until I reached the hotel did I realize that everybody had gone to the shelters. Being deaf, I had not heard the siren.'

A. F. G. heard the siren only too well, and has a constant reminder of it. He writes: 'We had not long been married, and were having a lie in a little later than usual as I had been on night work the previous week. I had been down and made a cup of tea and brought it up with the Sunday paper, which was full of all kinds of war news.

'The headlines frightened my wife, and I began to comfort her. As we were young, I suppose it was natural that the comforting should turn to love-making. Perhaps you are familiar with the opening of Sterne's novel *Tristram Shandy* in which he puts down his conception to his mother asking his father at the crucial moment if he had wound up the clock? Well, at my crucial moment, the siren went, with the result that when I came home on leave after Dunkirk I saw for the first time my son who was certainly conceived that morning at eleven-thirty. So long as you don't print my name, I don't mind your using this story.'

The first experience of an Alert had lasting effects on some people. Lieutenant-Colonel R. M. Trail recounts, 'I had arranged in my house in Iver, an underground "funk-hole", with oil lamps, tinned food etc., etc., for use if and when an enemy bombing attack should come.

'I was in my office at ten o'clock when it was announced we were at war and the sirens sounded. After the All Clear, I continued my work until about one o'clock, when I returned to my home expecting to find lunch awaiting me. But the house was empty and there was no sign of lunch.

'I eventually found my wife sitting in the dark funk-hole. She had hurried down on hearing the siren, shut the door and could not find the matches. She did not hear the All Clear and so sat in the dark until my return.

'For the rest of the war she refused to take cover until she actually saw the German bombs falling.'

Like Mrs Trail, Sir Brian Horrocks, (not yet a general, nor a knight, but an instructor at the Staff College at Camberley and feeling very anxious about the possibility of his being retained too long in what he considered a backwater) found his first experience of an air-raid shelter not to his liking.

'It was a nice sunny day,' he has written to me. 'My small daughter had gone riding. Suddenly we heard an air-raid warning and trooped down to a curious object that lay at the bottom of the garden.

'After a bit, we thought this was rather silly, and we came out again. We then heard the All Clear sounding and went back again, as we were not too clear of the difference between the two signals. This was the only time, as far as I can remember, that any of us was in an air-raid shelter during the war.'

Some of the wise ones who had taken precautions beforehand, had still not completed their preparations. Frank Edmonds's landlady was one of them. She had attended A.R.P. classes and had established a shelter in the basement, but had not provided the wet blanket over the door as prescribed, to counteract a gas attack.

'As soon as the warning went,' says Mr Edmonds, 'I raced up to my room, snatched a blanket from my bed, tumbled it into the bath and waited a few anxious moments whilst it became soaking wet. Then galloping down the stairs two at a time, trailing water all the way, the landlady and I fitted it over the door, getting our clothes almost as wet as the blanket doing so.

'Our discomfort was quickly relieved, however, by the sounding of the All Clear. As we went up to tidy ourselves up, we were met by a cascade of water splashing down the stairs.

'I had forgotten to turn off the bath taps. However, we were so relieved by the ending of the warning, we went to work to mop up the mess almost overcome with laughter. Later one was to meet everywhere people who were able to smile through tragic and harrowing moments.'

Mrs M. B. Rochester says, 'I do not think that any of the

bad things that happened in the following six years ever quite caused the awful fright that that first warning did. I was seventeen and getting ready to go for a bicycle ride with my first boy-friend when the siren went. For the first few minutes we all dashed around like demented things. I ran out to the shelter which my father had dug at the bottom of the garden and opened everyone's gas-mask box. I felt very foolish afterwards. Nothing has been quite the same since, not even the summers!'

For some that first warning has become associated with one special object, generally an article of food.

T. R. Rogers was mowing his lawn when the announcement was made and when the sirens went.

'Mrs Robinson, who lived opposite came bustling across to tell me we were at war. We were both in the A.R.P. so I told her to round up the other local members and go to headquarters where I would join them. When she had gone, I looked at my half-cut lawn. It looked very untidy, so I decided to finish it. I suppose Drake must have felt something that I felt when the Armada was sighted.

'The lawn finished, I majestically mounted my bicycle and went to H.Q. We had not been there long when a dear old soul came in carrying a large plum cake.

' "I can see them Germans coming over the Downs," she said, "so we may as well eat this now!"'

'One or two of us looked out, but could see no sign of Germans. But the old lady was adamant that we should share her cake. It was freshly baked, still warm and quite delicious. Since then, I have never smelled fresh-cut grass or eaten plum-cake without recalling that Sunday morning when war broke out.'

For Miss J. B. Kay the memory is of 'home-made Abernethy biscuits and butter, and children marching down a hill.'

'As Mr Chamberlain made his announcement,' she recalls, 'I stood by the window and watched the children from a nearby school marching down the hill to the railway station.

'Just as the Prime Minister finished there was a deafening peel of thunder and several vivid flashes of lightning. Our next door neighbours, who were not so young, came in very flustered. To calm them I made tea and brought out some freshly-made Abernethy biscuits and butter. They and my parents are gone now, but I never see Abernethy biscuits or children going down the hill without remembering that morning.'

Some people had taken no precautions at all, but decided to as the first siren sounded.

Sidmouth Willing was at his Sea Cadet H.Q. creosoting a sentry-box when the siren went. He decided to send the boys home quickly and went home himself. On entering the sitting-room, he saw two buckets of earth standing by the fire-place.

'What are these for?' he asked his mother.

'I don't know,' she replied. 'They got some in next door, so I thought I had better do the same.'

Mary Ireland set her family to work on gas-proofing the dining-room. 'We sweated at it all day,' she recalls. 'The meals were all late, and the day was a completely abnormal one. But our work kept us occupied. Needless to say, we never used the room for its intended purposes, thank God.'

At least one official department could not carry out its regulations.

Colonel Whitefoord was working in the German Section in the Directorate of Military Intelligence at the War Office.

'When the Alert sounded,' he says, 'all of us, as rehearsed shut windows, locked away secret papers, and taking the trays of papers from our desks, trooped down to the air-raid shelter—a room in the basement.

'However, we failed to get into our refuge; the official who had the key was off duty, as it was Sunday!'

The siren also ruined the proud boast of a certain news-paper office that its 'doors never closed.'

'As the Alert sounded,' recounts W. A. Bunce, 'several passers-by ran in for shelter. We were equipped only for our own staff, so a minor official ordered the main doors to be

79

closed and locked. When the chief proprietor arrived a little later, he was much upset about the closing, and issued a strict order that the doors must remain open whatever happened. And so it was throughout the duration and has been ever since, and will be until the building ceases to exist.'

In retrospect, and long before the war ended, many of the early beliefs and the regulations prompted by those beliefs, appear embarrassingly fantastic.

John Dowling was a Lance-Corporal in the Royal Engineers stationed at Chartham, near Canterbury. His unit had been moved to Shorncliffe to stand by for embarkation for France, and were accommodated in tents.

As the siren went, they were digging slit trenches between the tents. 'No one knew what to do,' writes Mr Dowling, 'and we stood gazing up, until the C.S.M. came running up shouting, "Don't look up men, or the pilots will see the whites of your eyes!"'

'Even on that first morning such a warning given in the middle of a large military camp easily recognizable as such from the air, gave us a big laugh.'

Sidmouth Willing, whose mother had laboriously filled two buckets with earth, repeated the experience of many.

'After I had set out for home,' he writes, 'within a mile I was stopped by a warden, who said, "Don't you know there's an Alert on?" He said no traffic must move and made me pull in to the kerb. Having sat there about ten minutes, I began to be anxious about my mother, who was in the house alone, so I produced my Special Constabulary warrant card and fibbed that I was going on duty. "In that case, you may proceed," he said. So I proceeded.

'Another mile and another warden hailed me. "Drive slowly, please." I acknowledged and reduced speed.

'In my home road, I was once again hailed by a warden, who called, "As quickly as you can, please!" I waved acknowledgement and complied. I often think I would have made a far more vulnerable target sitting in my car by the kerb or travelling slowly, rather than at speed.'

But it was all new. No one knew what to expect in actu-

1. H. M. King George VI sits alone in his study at Buckingham Palace and Broadcasts to his people: 'We are at war with Germany'.

2. A silent, unbelieving crowd watches as Big Ben strikes the fateful hour on 3rd September 1939. (Keystone Press)

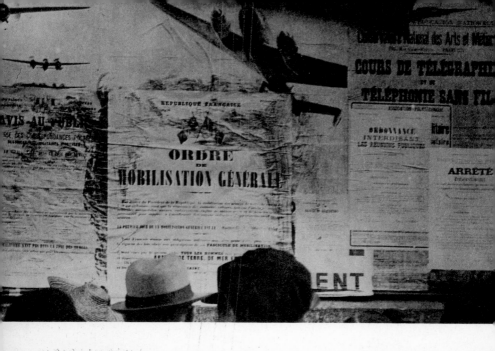

3. General Mobilisation orders for France and England following the invasion of Poland by Germany. (*Radio Times*, Hulton Picture Library)

4. *Above*. The first siren. People in Whitehall running to the nearest air-raid shelter a few minutes after Neville Chamberlain's broadcast that war had been declared. (Keytsone Press)

5. *Below*. Emerging after the 'All Clear' had sounded, shaken but relieved to learn that the alarm was false. (*Radio Times*, Hulton Picture Library)

The Daily Telegraph
and Morning Post

LONDON, MONDAY, SEPTEMBER 4. 1939

BROADCASTING—Page Six

BRITAIN AT WAR

WAR CABINET OF NINE

MR. CHURCHILL BACK AT ADMIRALTY

MINISTER OF HOME SECURITY

... MESSAGE
... EMPIRE

...LL FIRST LORD:
...OR MR. EDEN

...SETS UP WAR

A War Cabinet of nine has been set up on the lines of that established from December 10, 1916. It was established that the King had approved its composition as follows:—

Prime Minister and First Lord of the Treasury .... Mr. Neville Chamberlain
Chancellor of the Exchequer ..... Sir John Simon
Secretary of State for Foreign Affairs ..... Viscount Halifax
Minister for Co-ordination of Defence ... Admiral Lord Chatfield
FIRST LORD OF THE ADMIRALTY: Mr.

...LY MAIL. ...September 4, 1939.

The usual
...ONT PAGE
...ertisements
...ear to-day in
...Page 3.

HIS MAJESTY'S BROADCAST

The following message was broadcast by the King from Buckingham Palace throughout the Empire at 6 o'clock last evening.

In this grave hour, perhaps the most fateful in our history, I send to every household of my peoples, both at home and over-seas, this message, spoken with the same depth of feeling for each one of you as if I were able to cross your threshold and speak to you myself.

For the second time in the lives of most of us we are at war. Over and over again we have tried to find a peaceful way out of the differences between ourselves and those who are now our enemies. But it has been in vain.

We have been forced into a conflict. For we are called, with our Allies, to meet the challenge of a principle which, if it were to prevail, would be fatal to any civilised order in the world.

It is the principle which permits a State, in the selfish pursuit of power, to disregard its treaties and its solemn pledges; which sanctions the use of force, or threat of force, against the sovereignty and independence of other States.

Such a principle, stripped of all disguise, is surely the mere primitive doctrine that might is right; and if this principle were established throughout the world, the freedom of our own country and of the whole British Commonwealth of Nations would be in danger.

But far more than this—the peoples of the world would be kept in the bondage of fear, and all hopes of settled peace and of the security of justice and liberty among nations would be ended.

This is the ultimate issue which confronts us. For the sake of all that we ourselves hold dear, and of the world's order and peace, it is unthinkable that we should refuse to meet the challenge.

It is to this high purpose that I now call my people at home and my peoples across the seas, who will make our cause their own.

I ask them to stand calm, firm and united in this time of trial. The task will be hard. There may be dark days ahead, and war can no longer be confined to the battle-field. But we can only do the right as we see the right, and reverently commit our cause to God.

If one and all we keep resolutely faithful to it, ready for whatever service or sacrifice it may demand, then, with God's help, we shall prevail.

God bless and keep us all.

FIERCE FIGHTING ON TWO POLISH SECTORS

MANY WEEK-END RAIDS BY GERMAN WARPLANES

THRUST INTO EAST PRUSSIA CLAIMED IN WARSAW

Fighting on a more extensive scale is developing on both the main fronts in Poland.

The German attempt to cut the Corridor between Chojnice and Graudenz was reported in Warsaw last night to have failed. At the same time it was stated that the Poles had recovered certain of their towns in this zone and had penetrated across the border into East Prussia.

Further air raids were made on Polish towns over the week-end. A Polish Foreign Office statement estimates that 1,500, including women and children, have been killed and wounded by bombing since Friday.

Below are messages from our special correspondents in Warsaw and Katowice.

POLES CHEER DECLARATIONS

FROM OUR SPECIAL CORRESPONDENT
WARSAW, Sunday.

The Germans occupied Rybnik, Teschen, Bielsko and have reached the suburbs of Katowice. They are rapidly advancing on the Moravian Gate, and ...nications between Cracow ... ...ccurred at Cracow ...

Daily Mail

FOR KING AND EMPIRE

NO. 13,529   • • •   MONDAY, SEPTEMBER 4, 1939.   ONE PENNY

The King's Message to His Peoples

"WE SHALL PREVAIL"

Churchill First Lord in New War Cabinet: Eden at the Dominions Office

NAVY WILL CONVOY SHIPS AT ONCE

BRITAIN and France yesterday declared war on Germany. Both presented ultimatums to Hitler — he must withdraw from Poland or they would fulfil pledges to Warsaw. Both were rejected.

The British ultimatum was presented by the British Ambassador in Berlin, Sir Nevile Henderson, to Herr von Ribbentrop at 9 a.m. It expired at 11 a.m. From that hour Britain was at war.

The French ultimatum was presented by ...

King
...verv

THE King sat alone ... study at Bu... Palace yesterday an... cast a personal messa... people in their own hom... another room of the pa...

THE NEVER-SAY-DIE MOOD OF THE PEOPLE

In spite of Britain's unpreparedness for war—no Navy, no Army, no Airforce—they will still 'hang their washing on the Siegfried Line.' (with kind permission of the various newspapers, and the *Daily Express* for the David Low cartoon)

7. *Above*. Building an air-raid shelter, and for many of them their first taste of what war will mean. (Fox Photos)

8. *Below*. There it is! For the second time within twenty-five years. (Fox Photos)

9. *Above*. Herr Kordt, the German chargé d'Affaires, and his staff at the German Embassy in London about to leave for home. (*Radio Times, Hulton Picture Library*)

10. *Below*. Prime Minister Neville Chamberlain acknowledging the crowd's greeting as he leaves No. 10 Downing Street. (Fox Photos)

OWING TO THE
MANAGER BEING
CALLED UP THIS
SHOP WILL BE
TEMPORARILY
CLOSED

NEAREST BRANCH
6 BROADWAY
AND
75 FETTER LANE

11. *Above.* A sign soon to become familiar in every town and hamlet throughout Britain. (Fox Photos)

12. *Below.* Business as usual. The milkman delivers the milk that morning at No. 10 Downing Street. (*Radio Times*, Hulton Picture Library)

ality, and almost any criticism is too harsh. On the other hand, the lessons to be learned by Civil Defence from the behaviour of individuals should prevent similar recurrences should another crisis of such magnitude arise.

Mrs C. Ringer, nearly all of whose neighbours came to their doors to see what was happening when the first siren went, also relates that as they stood at their door, 'Suddenly one neighbour came running out of her house to another neighbour opposite with her gas-mask fixed firmly on her head. We all had to have a good laugh at the time, but we found afterwards that the woman concerned was extremely deaf, and had formed her own conclusion that there was a raid on, and therefore she must don her gas-mask.'

And Mrs J. M. Roberts has written to me, 'My family were at our seaside house at Middleton, in Sussex, and my son, aged eleven, had gone out on his bicycle. When the siren went he turned for home to meet an old woman wearing her gas-mask, who, in addition to presenting him with this strange and horrifying sight, gesticulated violently to him. She evidently wanted to tell him that he should do the same, but the sight so unnerved the boy that he rushed home, flung himself on the lawn and declared that he would not go out again till the war was won.

'This phrase of his also reminds me of another old lady who went into the village grocer's and asked confidentially, "Have you any Bronco?" "No," replied the grocer. "I don't think we shall be getting any now until the war is over." "Very well," she said. "I'll wait!"'

Surely the old and the infirm ought to have been the objects of special consideration by the authorities; and even the active and vigorous ought to have had the minimum of security procedure dinned into them.

Take for example, Alfred Paris's experience. 'Early that morning my wife, who was pregnant, and our three-year-old son had taken their places on the evacuation coach to the country and we had said our good-byes. I returned to my Chingford home and before long the banshee wail of that first siren began. Long before its last note had died out I was squatting under the stairs, as my only refuge, and as an

81

added precaution I felt it safer to put the white enamelled baby's bath over my head.'

Or that of Mrs Mary Chart, who has written, 'I was a Staff Supervisor at a large department store in Worthing, and at the request of the Town Clerk I had been released by my employer, with five others (all air-raid wardens) to act as billeting officers to the London children who were evacuated here.

'Council schools were used as centres and I was just about to pack six more children into the car and take them to a new home when Mr Chamberlain's voice came over the loud-speaker with the solemn news that we were at war. Then the Alert siren was heard, and we all looked at each other in wonderment.

'I left at once to report to my warden's post, and on the way met two young mothers pushing their babies in prams in great anxiety to get safely home. I did my best to reassure them, but they had no notion of what should be done in an emergency.'

While Robert Mitcham has written, 'I served throughout the war in the London Division of the National Fire Service. I had completed by part-time training before 3rd September and was called up on the eve of that date.

'I reported to the fire station at Eltham S.E. I was in the first crew to be sent out in charge of a regular fireman. We established a sub-station in one of the local L.C.C. schools. Many such schools were maintained as sub-fire-stations throughout the war in London.

'There were some eighty men subsequently stationed with me, and on the first night we slept in the small hall of the nursery school surrounded by dolls houses and rocking horses, and used the tiny trestle beds provided for the children.

'At about 2 a.m. we turned out to unload a lorry load of gravel from Blackheath, which was for sand-bagging. Throughout the day London taxis were collected from Brixton. These were used for some time as towing vehicles for the Dennis trailer fire pumps provided by the Home Office. They were an odd sight. *They had no towing bars and the trailer was hitched on with a length of* ROPE. The vehicles were filled with gear such as spades, axes, branches, stirrup-pumps and hydrant heads and shafts.

'At any rate, at my station each vehicle was provided with *only two lengths* of hose, and I very much doubt, if there had been a fire-raid, that much effective work could have been done.'

Even Members of Parliament had little idea how to behave. Duff Cooper and some of the members of his group had met at Ronald Tree's house in Queen Anne's Gate soon after breakfast that morning. There they listened to the Prime Minister's broadcast, and almost immediately afterwards set out for the House of Commons.

As they left the house they heard the sirens. They took no notice and walked on. Arrived at the House, they were ushered into a room opposite the downstairs smoking-room, which was already full of all kinds of people, including the Speaker and some of the staff. But they did not stay there long, but went up to the terrace to watch the balloons going up. Despite the Alert, the sitting of the House began as scheduled, and during the opening prayers the All Clear sounded.

Churchill has also recorded that when the siren went, he and Mrs Churchill climbed up to the roof to look at London. It had been given out by the authorities that between the sounding of the Alert fifteen minutes could be expected to pass before the arrival of the enemy planes. As this fifteen minutes ran out, Mr and Mrs Churchill went down to the shelter assigned to them, which was a hundred yards down the street.

They had been there for about ten minutes when the siren went again, and Churchill has noted in *The Gathering Storm*, 'I was myself not clear that this was not a reiteration of the previous warning, but a man came running along the street shouting "All Clear" and we dispersed to our dwellings and went about our business.'

The Prime Minister's announcement was to change the lives of every man, woman and child in the country.

H. Pratt had signed on in the Navy in 1913, and at 12 noon on 3rd September, 1939, he was due to retire on a pension after twenty-six years' service, At eleven-thirty he was called to his C.O. who told him that those due for retirement were being given the option of staying on for the duration.

'I fell for it!' says ex-Yeoman of Signals Pratt. 'The next six years proved the most hectic of all the thirty-two I served.'

It would seem quite clear, however, that three categories felt the effect more than most of the others—young wives, mothers of teenage sons and young children.

D.Y. says, 'John and I were glorying in every minute of our new lives as husband and wife, loving every moment of being together in our own tiny home. The threats of war had been only whispers to us, and so faint that our love-making only too successfully drowned them.

'Then came the awful day, and reality broke in on us roughly and violently. We were still in bed when the announcement was made. We had just finished demonstrating to one another the true depths of our love in a physical union that had made our senses reel, and were just coming slowly back to the room about us and the low sounds of the portable radio on the table on John's side.

' "I'll have to go," John said, holding me tightly to him and kissing me.

'I could not believe it, even when he got out of bed, shaved hurriedly and put on his uniform. I still couldn't believe it when he gave me a last kiss and went away.

'Stunned, I lay for a time not thinking at all. Then I saw John's clothes scattered about the floor. Still hardly realizing what had happened, I got up and began to tidy them into the wardrobe. Yesterday they had been clothes; now, all of a sudden, I realized they had another name—civvies!

'As I moved about the room, I kept repeating to myself, "He only joined the T.A. because he wanted to be in the band."

'When I had put away his tie and shoes neatly in the corner, still lost, I got back into bed. There the full meaning came to me. The bed was so awfully big. I jumped out and hurried from the room and sat down in the kitchen and cried. My mother called, and tried to comfort me. "War changes everything," she told me. How harsh and cold those words were.

'I'll never forget the day when something called ecstasy was snatched away from me, condemning me to perpetual pretence, for though John and I are together again that sudden wrench killed for ever my capacity to experience the deep pleasure and satisfaction of spent passion—but I must never let him know.'

For those who were about to be brides, the crisis was almost as much of a blow to their personal share of romance. We have already heard of the Palmers emergency wedding, and how, at a few hours' notice they got together cake and friends and persuaded the Vicar to marry them. Mrs Palmer has also related, 'At last we got ourselves ready for church and as we were waiting for the Vicar, about eight of our relations walked in with those horrid gas-masks slung over their shoulders. Then because there hadn't been time to get any confetti, we had hard, unromantic rice thrown over us—rice which later we would have given a fortune to be able to make into a pudding.'

Mrs D. Enefor says, 'The declaration of war cast a shadow over a wedding in our small village. Friends who were coming from London had sent word to say they could not come as their coach had been commandeered for the troops. The sweet shy young bride was all for putting it off and as she had been let down rather badly on her first engagement, seemed to think it was fate.

'I eventually persuaded her to "Damn Hitler" and have her own special day whatever happened. They are still ideally happy, so that is one thing Hitler failed to destroy.'

E. C. Sharpe was to be married, he writes. 'My girl-friend was relaxing in the bath with all the worry of preparations behind her—beautiful gown ready, six lovely bridesmaids, tiny girl and page-boy fitted out, catering done for eighty guests. The broadcast was out of her hearing and when the sirens went, they told her it was a practice.

'When the time came, the car arrived and took all the bridesmaids to the church, but no second car arrived for her. As time went on, in a panic she knocked at the house next door, and lunch-guests, who had arrived in a very old car, immediately jumped to the rescue, draped a clean sheet over the back and packed in the bride and all her yards of brocade.

'Her brother, who was giving her away, met her at the church. She was surprised to see him in a lounge suit instead of morning clothes, and when she asked why was told that the hire firm had closed shop. Still it did not occur to her that the bridegroom would be deprived of his wedding finery by the same cause until she caught sight of him at the chancel steps wearing his working clothes and a too bright, tatty tie.

'Then she remembered that his best new suit was at her home, waiting for him to change into for the honeymoon.

'It was a strange sight—the gloriously adorned bride, the beautiful bridesmaids, and the groom in his shabbiest suit. And only thirty guests arrived—but we've still got some lovely photographs.'

The feelings of mothers is summed up in these four letters.

The 3rd September was a fine spring day almost everywhere in Australia. G. B. Keele, of Myrtle Bank, South Australia, seeing how fine it was, suggested to his wife that they should go down to Victor Harbour for the day and have a crayfish lunch.

Mrs Keele recalls, 'So we all set off in our Ford V-8, my husband and me, our daughter Joyce, aged fourteen, our son David, aged twelve, and Margaret Cleghorne, a friend.

'We arrived there about twelve, and got a huge crayfish for three and six, and thoroughly enjoyed it. After lunch we heard the broadcast that England was at war with Germany. We thought, as did so many others, that it would last six months, and we'd have the Germans licked.

'That Sunday was the last day we had such a lovely trip for a long time, for petrol-rationing came in almost at once.

'My main thought that day was thankfulness that David was only twelve, and would not be called up. How wrong I

86

was! He joined the Navy when he was seventeen, but, thank God, returned safely.'

Mrs Gwladys Pelham was staying with a friend on a dairy farm about two hundred miles north of Sydney. 'As Mr Menzies told us that we were at war,' Mrs Pelham recalls, 'my hostess, who had four sons and a son-in-law at their spring camp doing military training, turned towards a photograph of the boys and knelt down and prayed. All five served overseas; four came back; the son-in-law was posted missing in Malaya.'

Mrs Mabel Joiner had come to the Old Country on a visit to her aged mother in April.

'My husband, my two sons and my daughter were in New Zealand,' she says, 'and my chief thought was—would I ever see them again? We had some difficulty in getting a passage, but sailed from Tilbury in November and arrived in New Zealand in December.

'I was glad to have got home, for my oldest son, who was not quite twenty-one, enlisted in April, and was sent overseas. I never saw him again. To my great sorrow, he was killed in action on 28th June, 1942. But if I had not had those last few months with him, my tragedy would, I think, have been so much worse.'

Mrs Dorothy Booth, who now lives in Salisbury, Southern Rhodesia, was at the time living alone in a house overlooking the sea at Joy Lane, Whitstable, in Kent, with three young daughters.

'We had been taught how to use the frightening gas-masks and expected gas-warfare immediately. We imagined ourselves to be very brave, and it was arranged that if the Germans suddenly arrived on our garden path from the sea, I should attack them with my husband's sword hanging conveniently in the hall. I half-believed that I would do this if such an eventuality arose, for somehow I had to protect my children.'

And the children themselves! Some took the news with a calmness which equalled any grown-ups, not because they did not realize what the implications were, but because they had faith in parents and in England's cause; some because they simply did not understand; some because it seemed to be a real-life adventure. Others took their cue from parents; others were surprised by events; while events washed over others because more personal experiences were dominant. Few were frightened.

Miss Theresa Lewis writes, 'I was fourteen and a half, and on a Country Holiday Fund holiday for poor children at Herne Bay, in Kent. It was with puzzled horror that we heard that war was declared. Another girl and myself were sitting on the cliff-top when the first air-raid siren went. To us it meant that death and the end of the world were imminent. Yet nothing happened. Lots of silence; lots of nothingness.

'Then I thought of the terribly large number of miles separating me from my family in London. Would I see them again? How could I save them, because I was sure that London would be the Germans' first target?

I rushed round Herne Bay, noting all the pretty bungalows for sale, knocking at doors, making inquiries about rents.

'Then I sent a telegram home saying, "Come immediately have found bungalow." Needless to say, my family hadn't panicked to the same extent as myself, and my fear subsided. My parents and little sister never came, and a week later, at the end of my holiday I returned to London and the phoney war.'

G. W. P. Spurway, now living in Salisbury, Southern Rhodesia, was fourteen and at home on holiday. 'As our house at Oakford, Devon, only stands a stone's throw from the church, my brother and I had been asked by the Parson, the Reverend E. M. Kelly, to let him know during the service what Mr Chamberlain said. Having heard the broadcast, we made a note that war had been declared and trotted over to the church. We handed over the note to Mr Kelly who was in the middle of his sermon and then went home having done our duty.

'On arrival at home, we saw that my mother was very upset at the news, having lost a brother during the First World War and presumably guessing that both my brother and I would one day become involved in this one. It was on that occasion that, as far as I can remember, I ever heard my mother swear. Though it cannot have amounted to much her anger was directed against a man called Adolf Hitler.

'We went out into the garden again, for it was one of those perfect cloudless days that one talks about but seldom experiences in England, quite unaffected by the news.'

Mrs Joyce Thompson was nine years old, and was on holiday at the Semens Convalescent Home at Ilkley, in Yorkshire. 'My mother, my small sister of five, and my grandparents were also there, but not my father, as it was not his kind of holiday.

'Early in the morning, on one of my usual explorations through the hotel I came across a man on the top floor who was perched on a high ladder sticking black cloth across the skylights. I asked why he was doing this, but do not think he answered.

'Then I went out onto the Moor as I was addicted to tramping alone and knew my way blindfold over the sheep tracks. My mother did not worry about me, as she knew I was happiest when alone with my own thoughts. However, when I returned, I believe it was around elevenses time, my mother looked anxious as the Matron had informed everyone that they must have their refreshments and then go to the recreation room to hear what the Prime Minister had to say.

'We children sat on the floor in front of the wireless set, our people on chairs behind us. Then we listened amazed as we heard that England was at war with Germany. When the Prime Minister had finished, the Matron announced that we must all go home immediately after lunch.

'We never took papers while on holiday nor listened to the radio and I sensed that my mother and grandparents were completely bewildered. The journey home to our town of West Hartlepool was a nightmare. I can recall no trace of fear for the future either in the voices or faces of my people, but my grandpa was most agitated because it was so dark, all the stations being blacked out and he was afraid we would go on too far.

'When we walked into our house it was unlike the home

I had left, as my father had improvised a blackout by covering each window with black paper. This was the first day we knew of the black-out. My sister and I hadn't the faintest idea that there was anything to be afraid of; there was only a sense of excitement.'

H. C. Beresford was twelve and attended a grammar school in an industrial district of Birmingham. On the Friday he had been evacuated to the country, to Evesham.

He recalls: 'On arriving at Evesham we were taken to the local grammar school and then split up into parties to walk to various districts of the town. We soon found that although the billeting officer had been very busy prior to our arrival, the number of householders who were prepared to take evacuees was less than the number of children who had descended upon the town.

'We walked up and down the main road of the town whilst the billeting officer pleaded with householders to take one or more of us. Finally there were just myself and another boy left, and as it was dusk, it was decided that we should return to the school and spend the night there. We were just leaving for the school when a woman approached and said that she had relented at the sight of us being turned away and would take us. She had no spare bed and was provided with a paliasse filled with straw, upon which we slept on the floor. The good lady was very worried about what her husband would say upon his return from work to find his family so increased—they already had two children and a lodger. She had no cause to worry for her husband was as kind as herself and we were made very welcome and comfortable.

'Although I had not been brought up to attend church regularly we were all made to attend on the Sunday, by our headmaster, who had come to Evesham with us. Sunday dawned bright and sunny in Evesham. Together with the rest of my school I attended the morning service at Bengeworth church, Evesham. The minister said a prayer for peace but we did not know then that war had already been declared.

'We were told, on arriving back at our billet, that war had

90

been declared. It seemed so unreal, not like anything I had imagined such an occasion would be. There was no great excitement and the lady of the house went on with her task of preparing the Sunday lunch.

'Outside it was just like one would expect a quiet country town to be like on a Sunday morning. I wondered what was happening at home in Birmingham and I felt cheated. I had not even heard Mr Chamberlain's broadcast. As far as Evesham was concerned, at least outwardly, there was no war and so it was until I returned to Birmingham a few months later.

'On reflection it does not seem possible that the day which spelled the end of life as we knew it between the wars, could have passed so uneventfully and quietly; yet that was how it did in my experience.'

William Turnbull was fourteen on this very day, and was staying with his late grandfather at Bude, in Cornwall. 'In those days one could buy a really extra-special bar of ice-cream for sixpence, and I had previously decided to celebrate my birthday by buying myself one of these giants instead of my customary twopenny one.

'The great day and I set off armed with my birthday present money, excited and determined to carry out my plan. When I arrived at the café on the beach which sold these ices, the counter was deserted. However, I noticed a large handbell used for summoning the staff, so I rang it vigorously.

'Minutes passed and no one came, but I was determined to have that ice-cream, and decided that the proprietor or his assistant would tire more quickly of hearing that bell than I of ringing it, so I rang and rang.

'Presently the ashen-faced proprietor came. "I heard you ringing that bell," he said, "But I've been listening to the wireless. The Prime Minister was on. He's just declared war on Germany, and that's more important than you and your ice-cream, my son!"

'Now it was my turn to be shaken. But feeling that there was nothing I could do about it, and that ice-creams would shortly disappear altogether, I paid my sixpence and bought

91

my "Special". Yet somehow, it didn't taste special, and instead of going off to play on the beach, I returned sadly to my grandfather's house ready to play my part in my London school's evacuation drill.'

Mrs K. Green, who lives at Ndola, Northern Rhodesia, was thirteen, and was living then at Sale, in Cheshire. 'I used to keep a brief diary, and I still have this little collection of childhood doings and thoughts. My entry for 3rd September, 1939 reads, "No Sunday School because war broke out."

'As a child I had been made to attend Sunday school fifty-two times a year, and this was a glorious holiday. My father was busy digging a 1914-1918 war trench in the garden with the help of neighbours. My sister and I attended a school run by two maiden ladies, who began filling sand-bags that day and supervising the strengthening their cellar so that the school could open on time. (They did not wish to lose any fees for lack of being prepared. In fact, we were one of the few schools which did open early in September, the Government schools remained closed until their shelters had been built.)'

Victor Hoad was eleven. He had lived in Brighton all his life.

'I had gone to visit my grandmother in Hove,' he writes. 'It was a part of Hove that was unfamiliar to me. It was characteristic of my grandmother to ask me to run an errand for her as soon as I arrived. She had run out of vinegar and asked me to go and buy her a bottle.

'It was a beautiful sunny day and I had wandered from street to street trying to find a shop that was open on Sundays, when I suddenly realized that I was lost. Several people were sitting at their windows taking the sun and as I went past one house a man wearing a cap walked past and seeing a woman sitting at the window, called to her, "War's been declared, Ma!"

'Young as I was, I had no knowledge of the political events which had led up to this, but something about the gravity of the man's manner affected me and I was very frightened indeed.

'I went from street to street trying to find my gran's house and presently I came to a place where some children were playing. The air-raid siren sounded and one of these children shouted to the others, "I'm going to get my gas-mask."

'At that time the distribution of gas-masks had not reached the part of Brighton where I lived, and I hadn't got one. Altogether this was too much for me and I fled home leaving gran to buy her own vinegar.

'On the bus going home the All Clear sounded and I noticed that everybody on the bus spoke to one another in a burst of that kind of relief that was characteristic of wartime England.'

For some of the tinies, the noise of the siren was frightening without their appreciating what it meant.

Dennis Trevelyan was crossing a school playground occupied by the Richmond A.R.P. when the sirens went. In front of him trotted a six-year-old girl, who, hearing the noise, turned screaming, and rushed into his arms, sobbing, 'Take me to my granny!'

'I did my best to calm her, put her down and took her hand,' he says. 'As soon as the wailing ceased, she was quite herself again and ran off home quite happily. A prophetic experience for both of us.'

B. A. Seward was in camp with twenty boy scouts in his charge. They had just finished the 'Scouts' Own' service, and were eagerly lining the bank of a nearby gravel pit ready to dive in at their scoutmaster's signal.

Before the shrill of Mr Seward's whistle had died away, he heard the wail of a distant siren. His first instinct was to call the boys ashore, then he realized that their splashing had drowned the noise of the alarm, so he decided to let them have this hour of freedom, and put his whistle up. There was no shelter within miles and he was the only adult present.

For him, however, the moment was more significant. To the east and south curved the distant London skyline, and he felt his gaze drawn to it.

'Quite literally,' he says, 'I expected to see London float away in dust and poison gas in a matter of minutes. When it did not, the relief was almost intolerable. For the rest of the day, I found myself glancing frequently in the capital's direction.'

To all lives war, we have said, brought changes. Life was never quite the same again, and for a very large number of men, and a lesser number of women, it meant, if not an upheaval, at least an upset quite out of proportion with anything continued peace could have wrought. Sometimes these changes were acceptable, sometimes they were not; but acceptable or not, they could not be resisted. Yet in all the evidence that has been placed before me, there is very rarely any complaint.

Consider, for example, the case of H. F. G. Treacher.

'I then worked on the railway—the Great Western—as a parcel porter at Reading station. Although it was Sunday, the company had everyone booked for duty as an ordinary day owing to the evacuation of London children.

'As 11 a.m. approached I watched the large clock on No. 1 platform. It was the end of England's time-limit for the Germans. Would it be war?

'I was soon to know, for in a short time, newsboys came on to the station selling papers with *War Declared* printed in the stop-press columns.

'Presently a train arrived from London, and a lady passenger who had evacuated herself, was changing at Reading, told me that the air-raid sirens had sounded as they were leaving Paddington station, the train was stopped and the passengers were given the option of walking back to the station or staying where they were. She said there were terrible scenes, barrage-balloons up and anti-aircraft guns in the streets.

'After finishing duty I went home and a car pulled up at the door. I was asked to report at Tilehurst first-aid post at once. Without stopping to change, I cycled over in railway uniform, and was taken then and there to help man the post, as I had been for some time a member of the St. John Ambulance Brigade and a part-time Civil Defence Warden.

'This day changed my life, for I volunteered for full-time Civil Defence and served through the Battle of Britain and on the coast for D-Day. I never returned to the railway, on which, in 1939, I had already completed twenty-two years service.'

Or the case of Mr Clifford Moss. 'I have always remembered that day and often relived it in imagination. As my wife and two girls are out and the boy is goggling at the T.V., I may as well use a few minutes in jotting down what I remember.

'I was a young graduate in Chemistry of Queen's University of Belfast, where my parents lived. Not clever, but endowed with some determination, I had worked very hard since I was fourteen and had won a scholarship to Queen's in 1936. In June 1939 I graduated with First Class Honours and was also top of my year.

'As my father used to say, "To them that have shall be given . . ." and as is the way of things, I also won pretty well every exhibition and studentship that was going. Two of these were of special interest—one a research fellowship in physical chemistry at Iowa State College, the other a minor affair known as the British Association Exhibition. The significance of the latter is simply that it takes the winner free to the annual meeting of the Association, which goes on for about a week, spanning the last few days of August and the first few days of September, usually.

'In 1939 the British Association was in Dundee and I reckoned there was just time for me to attend the meeting and then take ship to U.S.A. and Iowa, where the college year started, I think, about 15th September.

'So off I went to Dundee complete with a vast trunk, an enormous wooden box full of books—which my father (an amateur carpenter) had built specially for the U.S. venture —my golf clubs, oboe plus cor anglais set, and pretty well everything I thought might conceivably be needed during the several years in the great New World.

'Well, the meeting got off to a fairly normal start and everything seemed to be going according to plan. It's true that even we scientists were vaguely aware that the wireless and newspapers were making a bit of a fuss again about that chap Hitler and his goings on, but we'd had all that several times before and it wasn't until the Saturday that some of us began to get a little anxious that perhaps this time old Chamberlain really meant to have a show-down.

'You see, politics was not my cup of tea at all, and I am appalled nowadays to realize how abysmally ignorant I was in those days of what had been going on in Germany. Well, the Sunday morning came, and I went to the service in Dundee—the parish church I suppose it was. Shortly after 11 a.m. the vicar was handed a message. He interrupted the service and told us that Mr Chamberlain had received no response to his ultimatum and that consequently we were at war with Germany.

'He then resumed the normal order of service and the only outward effect of his announcement was that many women quietly wept, dabbing their eyes from time to time.

'It had been announced on the Saturday that the Association meeting would be terminated at once if war broke out, and during the Sunday most delegates left Dundee. What was I to do? Should I pack up and return home to Belfast? Or should I carry on in the hope of getting to America?

'I knew that many of my friends would be joining the colours immediately, though in my case "joining up" would mean some sort of war-time research work, I knew. While I wanted to do the right thing "for King and Country," I was terribly torn in trying to make a decision. The chance to do research in an American university was a dream come true, and would certainly not be repeated. Could I go for just a year, perhaps, and then come back and make my contribution? Or would that be too late to be any good?

'I spent the whole of that Sunday wandering aimlessly about Dundee trying to make up my mind. Visions of awful disasters befalling my family, with me safely on the other side of the Atlantic flashed before me. What if invasion should come, by air, or by sea, or both, in a matter of months, or even weeks? Would England yield in a few months, or would she close her ranks as so often before in history and fight back—even though ill-prepared—till one day victory would be hers?

'Gradually, as I thought and thought, the truth became

96

clearer to me. England would not give in easily, no bloody fear! She would fight against any odds that might be piled against her. After all, it had taken four years and more the last time and it seemed to me it would take as long or longer this time.

'As dusk was falling, I wandered down to the river bank, and there in the silent shadows of the great river, a submarine slipped quickly out into the North Sea. The Navy was heading out to meet the enemy, as so often in years gone by. British sailors would do their bit. British soldiers and airmen wouldn't give in so easily as that bastard Hitler thought.

'I would go to America for one year anyway and there would still be time to come back again and lend a hand, however small, to see the Jerries off. I went back to my digs with the decision made, and next day took the train for London and thence to Southampton and America.

'Well, it turned out not very different from that. I had a wonderful year of hard work and hard play and by May 1940 I knew I must return home, for things were getting tough—they had even had the cheek to bomb Belfast, a thing unheard of the last time.

'I reached Liverpool on 13th July and a few months later was posted to a research job connected with the atomic bomb project "Somewhere in England".'

The change wrought in the life of B.S. was tragic. He has written: 'I was married, thirty-eight, and had three girls aged eight, ten and twelve. For years I had worked for the League of Nations Association and the No More War movement and was a near-pacifist, for after experiencing the 1914-1918 affair I had no illusions about war.

'I went to church at quarter to eleven and during the service nothing was said about war, I felt really quite numb as I was sure war would be the news, but the numbness I felt was of disappointment that all the efforts of 1918 to 1939 had been wasted.

'This numbness was still with me as I walked home from church with my little daughter. I was sure that within a few days, hours even minutes there would be a shambles. On a bill outside a news-agent's shop I saw "War with Germany Declared". My little daughter said nothing.

'Back home I told my wife and I think we went out to a nearby school and drew gas-masks. The rest of that day I cannot remember. All I can remember is saying to myself, "Whatever happens life will never be the same."

'It never was. I was conscripted two years later, sent abroad and saw service in Italy and Greece. Returning in 1946 I came back to a wife so nerve-shattered by the war that she had to spend seven years in hospital. My adolescent girls all left home when my wife's mind went and have never come back. Now here I live at sixty-two, with my wife—her mental troubles cured—but my three children lost forever.'

For many ordinary folk the coming of war meant immediate separation from families for several years, though they were not, like D.Y.'s husband, called to the colours. There was Albert Bowyer, for instance who has written: 'At the beginning of the war, I had not long moved from my home in North Staffordshire to London and during the first week-end of September, had gone down to my old home to see my fiancée and my people, taking with me the inevitable gas-mask.

'On the Saturday evening I received a phone message from my chief in London, asking me to return at once to help organize a move of the office into the country the following day.

'There were hurried farewells to my folk. My fiancée's American cousin and her friend were worried to death because they had booked to return to the U.S.A. the following Wednesday. (They did manage to make it successfully.)

'I went to Stoke-on-Trent railway station to travel on the mail train to London at 1.20 a.m. on the Sunday morning. I left my own people and my then fiancée's folk working frantically making black-out curtains, so no one came to see me off.

'The mail train drew into the station from Manchester and already black-out precautions had been taken, for the train was in semi-darkness, small blue bulbs having been fitted in the light sockets, and the blinds were drawn. Many service men were returning early to bases from leave.

'I left the train at Willesden Junction at 6 a.m. on the Sunday morning. The sun was shining and I could not help wondering what the day would bring.

'I went on by electric train to Watford, where I went to my digs for breakfast, then hurried up to my office in London. Here we worked busily, packing current correspondence and cases into hampers for despatch to our hide-out; also all the office machines—typewriters, comptometers and the big Powers machines were similary loaded up to be sent away.

'Our work was interrupted when the sirens went for the first time. Remembering our drill, we trooped down to the basement from the fourth floor because the lifts were out of action, carrying with us our precious personal possessions. After a few minutes the All Clear went and we wearily toiled up all those staircases back to our fourth floor abode —it had all been a false alarm.

'The work of packing was finally concluded by about 4 p.m. and several of us were going on top of the lorry containing the office machines to X to help unload at the other end. We had to clamber on top of the machines, over which had been fastened sheets of tarpaulin.

'I was the last of the three to manage to get on to the lorry but, so eager was the driver to get away, that he started off before I could quite get into a reasonably safe and comfortable position among the crates and so on, and there I just hung on. All during that nightmare twenty-mile drive I kept expecting to roll off, especially when we took the roundabout at Mill Hill. Finally we got to our destination and I managed to get down, all stiff and sore. We unpacked the machines and other things from the lorry, then thankfully went our way.

'We stayed out in the country for eight years!—though I must say that in spite of the anxieties of war, we enjoyed all the sounds and sights of the countryside.'

Mrs M. Head was another of those uprooted from home and office. She has written: 'We were living at Purley, in

Surrey, at that time, and at the Law Courts in London, where I worked, we had been given sealed envelopes which contained information about the evacuation of our departments from London should war come. They were only to be opened in the event of the outbreak of hostilities, otherwise they were to be returned unopened.

'On that Sunday morning I was taking my mother and father for a drive through the country lanes to have coffee at Westerham. On the way to Westerham we heard the news, but we decided to go on and have our coffee, since we realized that it would be the last time we should be able to do so for perhaps a long time.

'So we drove along the roads, watched a convoy on the move, and eventually came to the little village not far from which Mr Churchill has his home. In the café, while my father ordered the coffee, I excused myself and went to the lavatory. I had the office letter with me, and I wanted to know what I was to do. I opened it and saw that we were being evacuated to Cambridge, and that I must report there next day.

'When the waitress had brought the coffee, I said to my parents, "I am being evacuated to Cambridge." My mother was a little upset, but my father thought it was a nice safe place to be sent to, and that cheered mother up a bit.

'We had our coffee, and suddenly as we were driving along a country lane, the first air-raid siren sounded. We stopped the car, as did some other people who were also driving along, and together with one or two small boys, we raced up a nearby hill-side and all crouched down by a ditch, in the shelter of a hedge, waiting for we knew not what. I well remember thinking as I crouched there that the Germans had not wasted much time. However, no bombs fell and we crept back to our car and drove home.

'Subsequently, we had closer contact with bombs and stray bullets. My father's factory in London was razed to the ground, leaving only two safes among the ruins, and he himself did not live to see the end of the war. He died worn out by the difficulties which confronted him every day. I stayed in Cambridge until the end of the war.'

Those few simple words spoken in his sad, disillusioned voice— '. . . consequently I have to tell you that we are in a state of war with Germany'—made of one of the unhappiest of British Prime Ministers a wicked fairy, though he himself was not responsible for the transformations which the waving of his verbal wand wrought in the lives of all those for whom he was responsible. It was unfair, grossly unfair, for a man who had fought for peace to be forced by an immeasurably evil man into condemning those who had put their faith in him, and whose faith he had tried, in his own fashion, to merit to personal upheavals from which they were never to recover, in the sense that 'life would never be the same again.'

3

Interlude - In the King's Other Realms and Beyond

IF THE KING was at war in one part of his dominions, was he not at war in all?

The links which bind the agglomeration of states, nations and peoples known as the British Commonwealth and Empire are still a constant puzzle to people who are outside it. They cannot understand how one member can disagree with and act independently of other members, and not only have their decision respected by the others, but have their right to the decision protected by those who oppose them. They cannot understand how in this family of nations there can be republics when the Mother State is a monarchy, republics, moreover, which accept the Monarch as the symbol of this strange unity.

The legal position of each member of the British Commonwealth is that each has the right to decide on its own foreign policy, as well as on all other questions effecting the good of their particular State. War is a political act, therefore any member of the Commonwealth had the right to decide for itself whether it should align its own foreign policy with that of the United Kingdom Government, or remain withdrawn from the conflict which the United Kingdom Government's policy made inevitable.

Be this as it may, however, the question asked at the beginning of this chapter, while being hotly debated in some parts of the Commonwealth, in other parts was merely a rhetorical question. The interpretation which was put on it was to govern the activities of the different administrations.

Australia and New Zealand had no doubts at all that the Crown was indivisible, and as soon as the news reached Canberra and Wellington that the Mother Country had declared war on Germany the two Prime Ministers took instant action to bring their countries to Britain's side. R. G. Menzies, the Australian Prime Minister, even went so far as to declare war without consulting Parliament; and Parliament subsequently upheld his action by a unanimous decision.

In New Zealand and Australia, they are twelve and ten hours respectively in advance of us in England. The news for these two countries therefore came late in the evening of 3rd September.

In Australia it was spring time, and John Reynolds, of Signdal, Victoria, was with fellow members of the Beechworth Ski Club, having a day's sport on Mount Buffalo. In the crisp sunshine and the exhilarating upward rush of air as he sped down the steep slopes, life was so good that no thought of war entered his mind.

After a hard and satisfying day's exercise, he came in the evening to his parents' home in Beechworth, and found them grouped round the radio, waiting for the important statement which, it had been announced, the Prime Minister was to make.

'From the moment Robert Menzies said we were at war,' he says, 'my whole life was changed. I made up my mind to join up at the first possible moment, and within a week or two I was in air force uniform, beginning a period of service that was to run to six years.'

The news that war had broken out brought feelings of shock though it had been expected, and the immediate reactions when the shock had worn off a little, were of deep regret and great determination. Though separated by the greater part of the world from England, the thought that the Mother Country was in imminent danger was uppermost in everyone's mind.

R. W. Jacobs, of Essendon, Victoria, says, 'My wife and I were listening to a radio play from a Melbourne radio station about eight-thirty when the announcer interrupted the programme to say that the Prime Minister was about to make an important announcement. We knew what was coming, but nevertheless we waited with a feeling of utmost seriousness for the P.M. to tell us that Great Britain had declared war on Germany, and that Australia would stand behind the Mother Country in her hour of trial.

'As an officer of the Australian Military Forces I knew I would eventually be called up to play my part, and in fact within a few weeks I was in camp training with the Forces. As a major in the 8th Division, I was with British, Australian and Indian Forces at the surrender of Singapore, and spent most of my three and a half years captivity on the Burma-Siam Railway.'

Some Australians were already involved long before the war broke out, and not only in their own country, on the training courses which the Government had introduced, but in the Mother Country itself.

H.H. of Melbourne was one of these.

'Early in 1939,' he says, 'a bunch of us kids, all pilots or instructors in clubs and flying school, heard of the need for flyers in Army Co-operation in England for day and night flying. Believing we saw here an opportunity to get in some really worthwhile experience and to lend a hand at the same time, we sailed to the U.K. On arrival a few of us were based on Croydon, myself among them, and the others all over the place.

'A few days before 3rd September, there was a panic on to clear all civil aircraft from the East Coast of England to any place in the West. Most of these aircraft were old crocks, but they were at least aircraft and flew most of the time.

'Anyway, no one seemed to know what the hell was going on, but we were told that someone had had the word to go to Cardiff, so we all wandered off at 3 a.m. for that place. We were all pretty well steamed up, and finding the hangers bolted and barred, we forced open the doors and as quickly as we could loaded the aircraft with lathes and all kinds of spares and got airborne. All seemed O.K. at Cardiff, except that most of us really ought to have been some place else.

'However, there was one old Dragon, a DH 83, left at Croydon. It was the old wreck that I had normally flown quite a bit and had some soft feelings for. To go back, two months before I had signed a contract with the Middle East Oil Company and was awaiting orders to fly an aircraft to that area and remain there. When things looked bad I asked to be allowed to back down on the contract and join the Air Force, but without success. So on 1st September I managed to bum a ride to London.

'Before leaving it was found that my old Dragon was still loafing at Croydon—and I was asked, could I please fly her over, as the oil company would not require me before the tenth. Anyway, I finally got to see the powers that be at Croydon, and after a helluva lot of yap-yap and phone calls to Cardiff, the O.C. said, "It's all right, so please get that thing out of here pronto."

'I was given a pass and wandered over to the hangar. The place looked deserted and I thought, "Hell, now my troubles really begin. It'll take hours to check and gas up!" Well, I found a box of tools and climbed up and looked around the skin of the top wing, etc., and checked the fuel tanks and found to my surprise that they were full. The oil was O.K., too.

'Then I heard some hammering from the old machine-shop and being somewhat startled I ran over and saw a bloke who didn't look English banging away at something or other. I stood there just looking and fiinally he spotted me and bowed slightly and said good morning, sir.

'When I found my tongue, I said, "Who the hell are you?" He took a deep breath and without a pause explained, "I am Carlo but that is not my real name I am a Persian and a trainee engineer and have been here six months but you never noticed me and I telephoned Cardiff and they said to service your plane fill it with any spares and some left behind to old and go with you I was with my girl for a week and missed the evacuation thank you sir."

'I couldn't help laughing. I told him that was fine, and asked how long he had been here and how he had got in, to which he replied that he had been at it for about ten hours

105

and had hopped over the fence as he always did. How he never stopped a bullet I'll never know.

'He went on to say that some thieving pigs from an opposition company had begun to strip the old girl and that there was no altimeter and no airspeed instruments in the i/panel. Well, he dug up the required instruments from a heap on the hangar floor and we fitted them in. He had already stacked in the spare parts and when I saw it all I nearly had the horrors. I said that if she lifted before the last hangar in take-off line, O.K., otherwise we would have to heave out a couple of boxes of tools.

'Well, we staggered into the air and as I turned I saw a Hurricane land and run on and hit a hangar and burst into flames (Croydon was small—"lumpy" is the only word for it.)

'It is so long ago now that I cannot remember the exact details, heights, etc., but I climbed up to an altitude to give me 1,500 feet clearance of the highest hills near Bristol way. We levelled out just on top of a solid layer of strato-cumulus cloud (8/8ths), and I do remember that my old Dragon seemed to be hurtling along at least 10 m.p.h faster than usual, though this was after quite some time. Then I kept constant airspeed and height, but slowly we began to sink into the cloud, or rather the cloud came up to meet us, which I figured was O.K. as the cloud would tend to be higher over the higher terrain.

'We were very slowly getting into the muck when I saw an R.A.F. aircraft along side and the pilot was making frantic signals or waving anyway. I waved back and he tapped his head with his fingers. Then I was strictly "in it" on instruments. I wondered if he wanted a recognition flare or something (we didn't have any, anyway) and I was slightly worried that he might take a shot at us.

'I guess it was twenty minutes later that I noticed the ever so white overcast we were in starting to darken and I thought, fine, we'll break under this stuff with plenty of ground clearance, because I'm still at the same altitude.

'Just then I looked around at my Persian "flight engineer"

106

to see if he was now awake. He started to smile and then his eyes became enormous and I saw real fear in them.

'He was looking over my shoulder ahead of me. I jerked my head around and I nearly passed out on the spot. In a second I saw a house coming at me and a field with its distant trees and fence running back up into the cloud. I hauled back and cleared the house and cut the switches and banged down on the lovely solid grass at a hell of a bat, but managed to stop a ground-loop. Though I had all my brakes on as far as they would go we ran right up to the distant trees.

'Sweat isn't the word for it. Poor old Carlo was covered in spare parts and odd tools. As I sat there trying to steady down, it took me several minutes to realize that the altitude was still happily registering our cruising altitude. Carlo took a look and gave the instrument panel one huge thump with a rubber hammer, and bingo, we found the needle showing our true height—2,000 feet odd. No wonder we had figured we had a fast Dragon, we had been very very slowly losing altitude and with the great load of spares we were carrying she had been pitching quite a lot and it was hard to figure correct speed exactly. Those were the days before a bomb like the Dragon was fitted with a sensitive altimeter or radio worth a damn.

'The best part of the story I reckon is, that while I sat and tumbled around in my pockets for a cigarette, Carlo had climbed out to inspect the undercarriage. (We had hit hard). Next thing there was a helluva row and a farmer had Carlo with his hands up and a .410 shot-gun in his middle saying, "You're not English, etc. etc.". Well, in the end, we managed to satisfy the old boy and he gave us tea and a shot of rum. I wanted to call Cardiff on the blower but we found that the war was on and the lines were being held open.

'It was quite certain that we would never get off the deck with the overload, so we dumped the spares in a barn to be collected by a truck later. (For all I know they are still there.)

'The sky cleared and we just made it over the hedge and staggered into Cardiff only to be told that the aircraft should not have been brought across anyway. There had been a mistake—the R.A.F. or someone wanted it.

'We had quite a party that evening, and a day or two later I set off for the Middle East, where I stayed a year before being released to join Ferry Command.'

On board the last British cruise ship at sea when war broke out were Mr and Mrs Allan Peters of Balwyn, Victoria.

Mr Peters says, 'On that day my wife and I were returning from a cruise to Port Moresby on the old Orient liner *Otranto*. It was a beautiful day, and Divine Service which was taken by the Captain was attended by a large crowd, and very impressive it was. The serious situation cast a gloom over all, and many wild rumours were being circulated.

'At 9.15 p.m. Prime Minister Menzies speech was broadcast over the ship's loud-speaker, announcing that Britain had declared war on Germany and Australia was standing by her. Most of the passengers were greatly affected.

'All visible lights were put out in the ship and portholes blackened, and the Captain ordered full speed for Sydney. There was a great crowd of anxious relatives and friends waiting for us at the Sydney wharves when we arrived there a few days later.'

Coming west with the sun, in India it was quarter to five in the afternoon as Mr Chamberlain was broadcasting at 11.15 a.m. in London. At a place called Bannu, in the northern part of West Pakistan—as it is called today—a young officer had been having an afternoon's tennis.

As he came off the court, he was told that a very important notice was about to be broadcast, and going into the club-house he joined those already grouped round the set, and with them listened to the news that Great Britain had, just a few minutes previously, declared war on Germany.

'We all considered it a great tragedy,' says this young officer, now H. E. Field-Marshal Mohammad Ayub Khan, President of Pakistan, 'and we reached the conclusion that somehow or other everyone of us would be involved in it, and that is how it turned out.'

On the Tilak Ghat on the Madras beach, at the same time, a militant Indian nationalist, President of the Indian National Congress, Subhas Chandra Bose, was addressing a large meeting. Among his audience was a young doctor, just qualified.

'As Bose was speaking,' Dr S. V. Joseph now recalls, 'there was a dramatic pause, as someone whispered something into Bose's ear. After a few moments, Bose announced that England had declared war on Germany, and went on to tell his hearers that the time had come for action against British rule.

'There was naturally a stir among the crowd, and many of them started dispersing a few minutes later, before Bose could finish his speech.'

Later in the war, Bose was arrested by the British for threatening to destroy the memorial to the Black Hole of Calcutta. He escaped to Axis territory, and it was learned that he had visited Hitler and Tokyo. On 21st October, 1943, he became the leader of a provisional government of Free India. He died after an air crash in Formosa in August 1945.

For W. H. Young, Warrant Officer Instructor in the Indian Wing of the Army School of Education at Belgaum in South India, it was a memorable day for three things which, at the time, seemed insignificant.

Mr Young writes: 'In August and September my wife and I were on vacation in Bangalore. In August I received a letter warning me to be ready to rejoin my unit at short notice because of the international situation.

'The radio soon told us enough and without waiting for orders we cut short our holiday on 2nd September. Next day at Hubli an Indian police inspector checked my credentials at the railway station. He said he had no information about the war. Further north, at Londa, a junction near and for Goa, Portuguese India, and an escape route for aliens, the European police sergeant did not appear to give us a second glance.

'Now, as far as I was concerned, it was the first time in my nine years in India that a police official who was an Indian had taken such action. He seemed a bit diffident at first, for Englishmen were not usually accosted in this way. But he did his duty.

'That was the first thing. Second, it was the first time that a European junior police official had appeared to avoid getting into conversation with me.

'Third, though our Station Commander was Brigadier Slim and it was not a universal feeling in those parts, I felt distinctly that the placid tranquility of the "Poonah days" would be shattered before we were through, and these feelings came from these two insignificant actions of two police officials.'

In a cutting a mile or so east of Seone station in the Central Provinces of India, there was a heavy landslide during the night of 2nd/3rd September, and the District Engineer, M. H. Davie, was supervising the clearing of the track.

'When he had completed the work,' writes Major Davie, 'the engineering train, without saloon carriages attached, steamed into Seone station at about 5 p.m. I.S.T. We were met by the local District Forest Officer, who asked us if we would like to come to his bungalow to hear Mr Chamberlain's broadcast.

'We accepted, and so it was that I heard the declaration of war in the bungalow in which Kipling had stayed while he was collecting material for his *Jungle Tales*.'

In the High Range Hills of South India, where there were many tea-estates all covenanted to British citizens, there was a small up-country club called Kandaly, where during the dry weather, estate managers and assistants foregathered with their wives to play golf and tennis, or to ride and afterwards to have a drink together.

On 3rd September, there was a larger crowd than usual at the club, and among them was S. G. Speer, who recounts: 'All the preceding week we had been tense with the knowledge that war was all but inevitable. During the morning the usual games were played and the tiffin-hour session at the bar lasted, as normal at week-ends, until about three o'clock.

'In a planting community, the pre-prandial beer and gin-time is generally when current topics are discussed with a vociferousness in direct ratio to the amount drunk. But on this Sunday, even the most callow of newly-joined assistants spoke thoughtfully of what war might mean to the members of our isolated community.

'The short afternoon siesta over, people moved out on to the tennis courts and golf links and within an hour or so the sudden twilight of India came down on the surrounding hills. The oil lamp was lit in the small main room and I and my wife with one or two others were sipping our first pegs of the evening.

'Outside on the veranda, there was a rattle of thrown-down golf-clubs, and Sandy came in. In the most casual tones he announced "We're at war," and went over to the bar and helped himself to a whisky.

'We looked at each other and listened quietly while Sandy told us the latest wireless news relayed to him by Donald who had just come down from his bungalow and was still outside telling other returning games-players about it.

'At the time I remember being conscious of a feeling almost of relief that the waiting was over, although I think perhaps I had dreaded the thought that it might come to this more than the next man.

'A good deal of hearty drinking took place that evening in the Kandaly Club and, I recall, some raucous singing of Tipperary and other old war songs. But there was an absence of vain-glorious announcements regarding precipitate enlistment because everybody knew that this time we had all been neatly docketed as Key-man, A-men, B-men and so on, according to our usefulness to the tea industry, and that not one of us could go before he was properly called up.

'Actually, it was a pretty ordinary evening, but as I look back on it now, seems remarkable. I think of the various characters as they came through the door from the veranda.

'Sandy, the bearer of the evil tidings, went into the 5th Mahratta Light Infantry and, as far as I know, did not have a very strenuous war. At one time he was commanding a detachment of his Sepoys in the Seychelles Islands and there found himself a charming French wife whom he brought back to the district after the war.

111

'Norman, who followed Sandy in, swinging his tennis racket, two years later was captured with some of his fellow officers and men of the 5th Battalion, 7th Rajput Regiment by the Japs amid the ruins of the blazing docks of Hong Kong.

'A small cheery fellow in flannels came in next. This was Colin, not long out from the London office. His Artist Rifles blazer bespoke the keen amateur soldier. He made a keen and brave young officer in the Indian Army and about four and a half years later, serving with the 6th Rajputana Rifles, was killed at Cassino.

'Bill and Eric arrived together looking pleased with themselves and poured out mugs of beer. I think Bill must have had some fore-knowledge of what would be happening to him two years later when he had his company of Sepoys of the 10th Baluch Regiment would be opposing stronger forces of Japs on a jungle hill-top in Burma, though he could not have seen the long months he would spend in Rangoon jail as a prisoner of war.

'His Australian wife, Bron, who was sitting with us, could not know that a couple of years later, ignorant of whether her husband was alive or dead, she would be running single-handed, Bill's mother's coffee estate in the remote Shevroy Hills.

'Eric became a Gurkha officer and I believe served most of his war in the Middle East.

'George, who came in next, was to be first away to the war and within a very few months had also donned the wide-brimmed hat of the 7th Gurkhas. Before long he had received a bullet in the thigh, and, when things went wrong in Burma, was to be seen cheerfully swimming the Salween River with the aid of two empty petrol tins.

'Ken then appeared and made for the bar. He had never seen a glider then, but before peace came, he would have flown in one, with half-a-dozen mules as his companions, and crash-landed in an Upper Burma paddy-field with dozens of other aircraft supporting Wingate's Chindits.

'Dick and Kit, who followed, both within a few months were the other side of the Arabian Sea, one in the Gunners and the other in a Punjab Regiment fighting the Italians in Abyssinia and Somaliland.

'The Middle East was also to see the other members of their foursome, Lindsay and Percy, who in no time at all, were subalterns in the 7th Rajputs and in action at Sidi Barrani and elsewhere on the North African Coast.

'There were others present on that eventful evening, but who they were I have forgotten now. They by no means represented the full total of those in the High Range who would find themselves a considerable distance from the mountains of Travancore before they were much older. I doubt if more than one or two of those young men and women at Kandaly Club that night were destined to see England again within seven or eight years, which meant a lot of them had done ten years away from Home before they got back. As I have told, some never got back at all. Of course, none of us knew this would be, none of us knew anything except that this was it and the future would have to take care of itself.'

Miss Alice R. Veeraswamy, of the A.B.M. Girls' High School, Nellore, had been visiting the United States and was on her way home in an Italian liner. In a long letter which she wrote to all her friends in the New World, she said: 'The newspapers at Aden gave us the first warning of the tense international situation, but it did not scare us in any way. I went ashore and had an interesting visit with some Indian merchants who were most generous in their entertainment.

'For two days after we left Aden the boat shot up and down the billows and rocked from side to side. Except for a handful of well-balanced individuals, the crew as well as the passengers stuck to their cabins.

'On 28th August the boat was expected to touch Bombay. I was all ready to step off the boat the previous day. Some of us who were to land in Bombay planned to sit up the whole night to catch the first glimpse of our home-land. Only those who have turned their steps homeward after wandering on a foreign strand, can imagine how fast our hearts beat as we thought of seeing India once again. Only

113

then could I understand the mad yells of the American passengers on the s.s. *Bremen* on 20th September, 1937, when they saw the skyline of New York and the gleam from the statue of Liberty and broke into that song of the Star-Spangled Banner.

'At noon when the happy crowd gathered in the dining-saloon, the emergency bells rang, and it was whispered that the Captain had an important announcement to make. All of a sudden the merry laughter ended and everybody's attention was directed towards the Captain. What he said I could hardly hear, but one thing I understood; that we would not reach Bombay the following day.

'It was a blow indeed—one that came like a bolt from the blue. Studying just one group of people gathered on the deck after this announcement, I could see the different types of reaction to calamity.

'From 27th August till the 3rd September, we just sailed on and on, not knowing whither we were bound. All that we could see was just the vast expanse of water and the blue sky. Only from the rising and setting sun could we guess in what direction we were sailing. There is sound philosophy in this—that any woe shared by many simultaneously seems to lose its keenness to some extent. Each tried to comfort and amuse the other. Often in times of great uncertainty and peril, while I sat on the deck too dazed even to think, those challenging words of the Psalmist came to my mind over and over again.

> Whither shall I go from thy spirit,
> Or whither shall I flee from thy presence?
> **If I take the wings of the morning**
> And dwell in the uttermost parts of the sea,
> Even there shall thy hand lead me,
> And thy right hand shall hold me.

'On the fourth day of our endless wandering we were allowed to send radio-grams to our folks, but we had no choice in the messages to be sent. This was the prescribed form—"Well, arriving late". But even this was consoling.

On the 3rd September one could hear shouts in different

114

languages at the sight of land. Our joy was similar to that of the men of old under Xenophon when they caught a glimpse of the Black Sea or the crew of Columbus when they sighted the shores of America. We were aching to go ashore when the boat drew near to the port of Batavia, Dutch East Indies, but the pleasure was denied us. We were soon on the high seas once again. The hope of landing in Singapore the following day kept our spirits buoyant.

'The trip from Batavia to Singapore was the most picturesque part of the whole voyage.

'On 4th September, the ship docked in the harbour of Singapore. Even before I went down the gangway I could see in huge headlines the declaration of war from the newspapers sold in the harbour. And then I knew why we had wandered so far afield. The Captain had been afraid that if war broke out while he was in Bombay, his ship would be seized. And what sad news!'

In Aden, the strategic colony on the south Arabian coast, two hours west from India and three hours east from London, a strange thing was happening.

C. B. Martin, a marine engineer, had arrived there a few days before to join a ship which was on its way to the port.

'As I was the only unemployed officer in the place,' he recalls, 'I was co-opted into several jobs, mostly to do with rewiring rooms for telegraph censors and with minesweeping.

'On the afternoon of 3rd September, about three o'clock local time, or midday London time—we had heard the Prime Minister declare we were at war—a cruiser appeared in the roads with number and distinguishing flags flying. As she approached, to our surprise, one of the shore batteries fired a warning shot across her bows, but she sailed serenely on and moored inside the harbour.

'Apparently the cruiser was flying the correct code flags, which had been changed the previous night, but had not been communicated to the battery. I have often thought it strange that the only shot fired in Aden during the Second World War should have been at one of our own ships.'

Edward Carlisle was up the Red Sea from Aden, in the port of Suez. 'We had arrived there on the evening of 2nd September in the s.s. *Largs*. It is, in retrospect, a most significant thing that the Captain never allowed the ship's radio to broadcast at any time during the trip, until the inevitable 3rd September, when we heard the miserable statement of Chamberlain.

'Throughout the day we sailed slowly and silently up the canal and in the evening came to Port Said, where the newspapers were full of the potentialities in connection with the neutral countries which adopted such a negative attitude to such a positive reality.

'The passengers were vehement concerning the "ifs" and "buts" and many booked their passages back to Australia when they were able to see our diplomatic people in Port Said. Personally the thought never occurred to me. I took a fatalistic view of what will be, will be.

'The Italians, who occupied prominent buildings on the sea-front, were compelled to leave them, we were told, because they would not conform with the black-out regulations. It was a place as depressing as the news, and I was glad when evening came and we slipped out into the Mediterranean heading for Malta.'

To the north of Port Said, in Jerusalem, capital of the British Mandated Territory of Palestine, Mrs Nora Blaze sat on her balcony overlooking the German Legation.

'As I sat there,' she recounts, 'I wondered what would happen to the large German colony in Jerusalem. They must have had no such doubts, because within a few minutes of the declaration of war being announced over the radio, suddenly the air became full of tiny particles of charred paper. They were already burning their secrets, and none too soon, for before the day was out, they had all been interned.'

Unlike the Governments of New Zealand and Australia, the Government of the Dominion of South Africa was in no hurry to declare war. The Prime Minister, General Hertzog, was openly pro-Nazi, and on hearing of Great Britain's declaration, the old man told Parliament: 'This war is be-

116

tween England and Germany; it has nothing at all to do with South Africa. We shall treat Germany as we will treat *all* other belligerents.'

Fortunately there were others who thought differently, and equally fortunately, they were led by a man of outstanding courage, determination and statesmanship, Jan Christian Smuts, Deputy Prime Minister.

It was fortunate, too, that the Union Parliament was in session, having been recalled to prolong the life of the Senate for a further year, owing to the serious international situation.

P. V. Pocock, the South African writer and for twenty-nine years a Member of Parliament, has thrown an interesting side-light on this fateful day.

In a letter to me he says, 'I was staying at the Civil Service Club in Cape Town, and among the other guests were Colin Steyn and J. Hirsch—like me, both M.P.s—General Smuts and Louis Esselen, ex-General Secretary of the Party, a Railway Commissioner.

'That Sunday morning the four of us, excluding General Smuts, hired a car and motored on the Darling Road, where we stopped for a while to gather wild flowers. On the way back to the club, we heard Neville Chamberlain's broadcast.

'We went straight to the bar at the club, and while we were enjoying a drink, General Smuts came in and asked us what we had been doing. We told him, and as General Smuts was a keen botanist, we offered him the wild flowers. He thanked us and saying what great pleasure they would give him, took them up to his room to study.'

After lunch Smuts attended a Cabinet meeting at the Groote Schuur, at which General Hertzog announced that he was going to declare South Africa neutral. Smuts immediately opposed him, but Hertzog was confident that he would carry a majority in Parliament.

The rest of the day Smuts went quietly about among his friends and supporters, and when he followed the Prime Minister in the Lower House next day, he spoke with such quiet effect that Hertzog's motion was defeated by eighty votes to sixty-seven.

117

Despite this, the Prime Minister refused to resign until called upon to do so by the Governor-General, who asked Smuts to form a Government, and in doing so, provided England with one of her staunchest allies.

The 3rd September in South Africa was a day of tension for the majority of ordinary people, not on account of their Government's odd behaviour, but because they, too, were fearful of the fate of the Mother Country.

In the preceeding weeks, the father of L. E. D. Winchester of Durban, had daily lectured his sons on the horrors and futility of war, recounting to them his personal experiences in the First World War, and in particular at the Battle of Mons.

'If war comes again,' he declared roundly, 'none of you boys is going. I hope that's understood.'

'On that Sunday,' says L. E. D. Winchester, 'I was playing League cricket in a suburb of Johannesburg and on my way home after the game, I learnt of the outbreak of war from people standing on the street corners.

'For the rest of the way, I pondered what we boys could do to persuade my father to change his mind, for it seemed to us that England would need all the help she could get.

'I had expected to find my father at home, and asked my mother where he was.

' "He's gone!" she said.

' "Gone where?" I asked.

' "To the recruiting office! As soon as he heard the news, he couldn't wait to join up—if they'll have him at his age!" my mother said.

'I was struck speechless. After all he had said. . . ! Then I realized that he had planned it all along. He wanted to be the first of the family to volunteer. The Army did take him —he was one of the very first volunteers in the whole of South Africa, and eventually all of us boys followed him in. I personally spent the last year of the war as a P.O.W. after being shot down over Warsaw.'

Bert Abrahamse of Cape Town had not got to bed until 3.30 a.m. that morning. He was a musician and had been out on a professional engagement.

His wife had been put out by his very late return, and had left him in no doubt about what she thought of him. However, by morning she had calmed down, and at ten-thirty she woke him to tell him the news.

'I got up and went downstairs,' Mr Abrahamse has written, 'because though we had been expecting it for days, now it had happened it required an effort to take it in. But there was no doubt that it was real.

'Most of the day I sat by the radio listening to the extra bulletins and news-flashes. At five in the afternoon the *Cape Argus* brought out a special four-page war edition, and seeing it in black-and-white seemed to drive it home as none of the broadcast news had done. But the thing that really worried me was what our Government was going to do.

'Surely they must go to England's help! Why hadn't they said so already?

'My question was still unanswered when I went to bed, and I suppose my feelings must have been very like those of the people of England on the Friday and Saturday when they wondered when their Government was going to honour its pledges to Poland. It was this which affected me more, I think, than the fact that England was now at war.'

In Benoni, George Rennie, the former mayor, had not waited for formal declarations of war. Two or three days before, he had issued a call to all old soldiers to attend a meeting on Sunday morning, bringing with them what arms they could raise. Among the men who responded was Richard Davis.

'About a hundred of us turned up,' he says, 'but before we could fall in on parade, three police officers arrived and told Mr Rennie that armed parades were forbidden. After some talk, we had to disperse, and when we got home we heard that England had declared war. We might not have had our meeting, but at least a hundred of us were prepared if England should need us—and she did.'

To the north of the Union, in Southern Rhodesia, there was no reluctance on the part of the Government, no desire to prove independence, only a fierce desire to be at England's side from the very first moment, a desire which was translated into action by a declaration of war within a few minutes of England's own declaration.

Miss Moira Slater of Salisbury, was spending a few days with two friends at Rhodes Inyanga Hotel. The Inyanga Estates are part of Rhodes's great legacy to Rhodesia. The hotel was a simple one, surrounded by fruit orchards and forests of pine and oak.

Recalling the moment of England's declaration, Miss Slater writes, 'It was a strange scene in that tiny hotel sitting-room, crammed with people from the hotel, bronzed foresters, farmers, an elderly couple holidaying, a young policeman and his bride on their honeymoon, ourselves and many others.

'There was a profound silence in the room as Mr Chamberlain told us that once again Britain was at war. We all rose to our feet at the first drum roll of the National Anthem, and remained standing to hear the sad tones of the King speaking to us.[1]

'Someone stretched out his hand to switch off the radio and then the silence was broken by the elderly man saying to his wife, "I'll go and pack and see if they can give us an early lunch; you need not leave, dear, but I must." Of course she went, too. The foresters drifted to the bar to talk it over and decide what to do. The young policeman and his bride and we, too, went to ask for an early lunch, and then dispersed to pack.

'On our way to Salisbury, we stopped for a rest at Russape Hotel, and the young man left his wife weeping at her table and came across to tell us that he had been recalled to his unit. Our hotel was crammed with men "on their way". I heard one tall man call across to a friend, "Hullo, old man, what are you going to do about it?" and the answer, "I've sold the farm and am off to England tomorrow."

'All over Rhodesia scenes such as this occurred, showing the intense fervour of the spirit of love for and loyalty to the Motherland that swept through the people of Rhodesia.'

[1] Miss Slater's memory is slightly at fault here, the King did not broadcast until the early evening.

120

Anthony Heron of Marandellas, Southern Rhodesia, was a learner telegraphist in the G.P.O. at this time.

'I began to feel the excitement of call-up,' he writes, 'when during the middle of August six telegraphists joined the Rhodesian Air Force and were sent to patrol the border of Abyssinia and Kenya. A friend of mine, Mickey Payne, who worked on the Cable and Wireless Ltd., would pass on any news he had picked up from London operators, so I felt that the war was imminent.

'The 3rd September being a Sunday, as usual I went to Holy Mass with Cyril L'Estrange, a very good friend. It was after Mass that we knew that Chamberlain had given Hitler until 11 a.m. to withdraw his forces from Poland.

'We discussed the matter amongst ourselves, but we felt that Chamberlain would not go to war, though we hoped he would not back down.

'As 11 a.m. B.S.T. is 1 p.m. Rhodesian time, we ignored our lunch until after listening to the B.B.C. news, and Chamberlain's declaration of war. Within minutes, our Governor, Sir Hubert Stanley, and our Prime Minister, Sir Godfrey Huggins, declared war on Germany. Southern Rhodesia was the first self-governing colony to declare war after Great Britain.

'After lunch I went with a party to Hunyani Hotel, twelve miles out, where we had a few drinks to celebrate. I was only eighteen then, and war appeared an exciting adventure. After a few drinks at Hunyani, we returned to our digs and had a quiet supper. I shared a table with a German, John Boell, and I can still remember his remarks.

' "War is not fun," he said. "Soon you will regret your joyous celebrations. War can only bring misery to us all." Though he had to report regularly, to the police, John Boell was never interned.

'After supper I teamed up with Cyril L'Estrange, Ronnie Evans and "Tort" Fothergill and Ted Smith and several others to see a film at the Palace Theatre. I cannot remember the name of the film, but I will never forget "Tort" Fothergill jumping on his seat and singing *God Save the King* during the showing of the British Paramount Newsreel.

121

"Tort" survived the war, and ended up with a brilliant record as an artillery officer. If war came now I would not greet it with such light spirits as I did the beginning of the Second World War.'

R. A. Scammell was a guest at the Imperial Hotel, Kampala, Uganda, on this day.

'I was walking over from the hotel annex, a single-storey wooden structure containing single bachelor-bedrooms, when I ran into Tighe, a Power Company's linesman, who occupied an adjoining room.

' "Hey!" I said, "you drunken beast, you kept me awake most of the night with your fumblings and thumpings round your room."

' "What do you mean?" he asked. "I was out on the Kampala/Masaka powerline all last night. I've only just got back."

' "In that case," I told him, "there must have been somebody in your bedroom."

'He still looked puzzled, and then suddenly he began to grin. "I know," he said. "It must have been that snake of mine in its box under the bed."

'I was in no mood for jokes, so I went on with a mumbled comment. As I entered the hotel lounge, King George was just beginning his broadcast. In a foreboding mood, I left the hotel later, and passed Tighe on the annex lawn supervising eight lusty Buganda boys straining to hold outstretched a fourteen foot python, while Tighe argued with a Hindu shoe-maker the price for its skin. So he had not been joking.

'I registered only a momentary feeling of irrational annoyance. I had much more serious things on my mind.

'Forty-eight hours later I had been called up, and was on the night mail train for Nairobi as Volunteer No. 347 (Uganda Platoon) Kenya Regiment T.A. I met Tighe later during the war and learned that he had settled for his python skin at £8.'

In Ottawa, the capital of the Dominion of Canada, people were only just stirring awake as Mr Chamberlain made his broadcast. Mackenzie King, the Prime Minister, however,

122

had been up since the very small hours, not that he intended to do anything—just yet. He had been Prime Minister for nearly fourteen years and was proud of his country's independence. How independent Canada actually was, he was now determined to demonstrate. No one should be able to say after this that Canada was tied to Westminster's apron-strings.

So he did not declare war until 7th September, and the Order in Council making the declaration effective was not signed until three days later.

But the delay, besides showing the world how independent Canada was, had its decided advantages.

In 1937, the United States had passed a Neutrality Act, one clause of which debarred the Americans from supplying any nation at war with arms. The United Kingdom and France had both placed considerable orders for arms with American manufacturers, and so had Canada. Fortunately, nearly all the French and British orders had been delivered by the beginning of September, for as soon as the two countries declared war on Hitler, the operation of the Neutrality Act cut off all further supplies.

Now, although the Canadian Government was in no hurry to make its formal declaration of war, on 1st September, the day on which Hitler marched into Poland, under the powers vested in it by the War Measures Act of 1914, the Canadian Government had declared 'a state of apprehended war.' This permitted the country to begin to take all measures of a preparatory kind, and in effect gave a warning of intention.

Exactly what Canada's position was, was not clear to the State Department in Washington and President Roosevelt, and it was important for the Americans to know whether Canada was also debarred under the Neutrality Act from receiving arms shipments still due to her. In President Roosevelt's view the question could be settled by asking Mackenzie King to state categorically, one way or the other, what Canada's position was legally under 'A state of apprehended war.'

Cordell Hull, the Attorney-General and one or two others

were in the President's study conferring with him on the many domestic issues which automatically arose from the outbreak of war in Europe when the President suggested that Mackenzie King should be asked. They agreed that this would be the best course, so the President, always a man of action when action was needed, at once lifted the telephone and asked to be connected with the Canadian Prime Minister.

Mackenzie King was in his office in the east block of the Government Buildings when the call came through.

'Are you at war?' Roosevelt asked him.

'No,' replied Mackenzie King. 'We shan't be until Parliament says so.'

'But you intend to declare war?' asked Roosevelt.

'Certainly. I have called Parliament to meet on 7th September for that purpose,' Mackenzie King told him.

'But until that happens you are not legally at war?'

'Correct,' affirmed the Canadian Prime Minister, and heard Roosevelt say to those with him—he was speaking specifically to the Attorney-General—'You see, I told you so.' Then to King, 'So we can continue sending you arms until the 7th.'

'Probably longer than that. Parliament will pass a motion that war should be declared, but before we are actually at war the King must sign an Order in Council to make that decision effective. This won't be done until two or three days after Parliament meets.'

'Right. Thanks,' said Roosevelt and rang off.

During the next week the arms deliveries to Canada, on the President's express instructions, were greatly speeded up, so that by the time Canada was officially and legally at war, she had received all that was due to her. This proved to be a great advantage not only to Canada herself, but indirectly—may one hint directly—to Great Britain.

There were, of course, Englishmen in Europe on this day. One of them was J. R. Shotton, who happened to be in Belgrade.

He recalls: 'On this Sunday there were motor-car and motor-cycle races being held in Kelemegdan Park, Belgrade. I was invited by another Englishman, Mr Litvinne, to watch

124

the races from his apartment overlooking the course. I remember there were several German competitors.

'For obvious reasons, we had the radio tuned in on London, and it was during an interval between races that we heard Neville Chamberlain say ". . . in consequence of this, this country is at war with Germany." When the National Anthem was played at the end of the Prime Minister's announcement, both Mr Litvinne and I joined in.

'The Yugoslav post office issued four stamps on this day. I have them in my collection.'

Arthur Mackerras was in Berne on business. 'To say that the news that war had been declared came as a shock would not be accurate, and yet, at the same time, it was a shock. It is very difficult to describe. My first thoughts were, How well is England prepared? Have we enough trained men, suitably armed, to send against this powerful enemy?

'I think these thoughts were, in the main, provoked by events that had happened in Switzerland in the past week. True the Swiss Press had been non-alarmist during the weeks before the crisis, and had reported objectively from both sides. True they had emphasized that whatever happened, Switzerland would maintain her traditional *rôle* of strict neutrality. And yet, on the previous Sunday, 27th August, a strange event had taken place—the Federal Council had met, which it had not done on a Sunday in many years.

'What is more, the Council had met to take a great decision: That a General should be appointed to lead the Swiss Armed Forces.

'I should explain that in peace-time, the highest rank in the Swiss Army is Colonel, but in times of crisis a Commander-in-Chief is appointed. He is given the rank of General, and retains this rank only so long as the crisis lasts.

'Three days later, the Federal Parliament met to carry out the Federal Council's decision, and a certain Colonel Henri Guisan was elected to be General. But even before the General was appointed, the Federal Council had called up 100,000 men of the special frontier troops.

'It was a most extraordinary thing that this little country, which had not been involved in a war for the last seven hundred years at least, should take these precautions before war had broken out; but as I wandered about the clean Berne streets in the warm September sunshine on this morning, and saw young Swiss men in uniforms hurrying about their tasks, it gave me a feeling of reassurance.

'If, I thought, the Swiss, who are unlikely to be involved in war, have had the foresight to take precautions to meet a non-existent enemy, surely the British and French Governments, who must have known that war with Hitler must come one day, will be ready to meet and defeat him. Since then, and in the light of the experience of the next six years, I am glad that I am not a clairvoyant, for if I had known what lay ahead of us on that September Sunday, I don't know what I should have done.'

In Copenhagen, it was also a bright, sunny morning, and Duus Agerbak was strolling in the Luna Park when he was told the news by a friend whom he met.

'When the British and the French had not declared war on Germany the moment Hitler attacked Poland, we had begun to wonder if the Western democracies had any intention of fighting at all, especially when, on the Saturday, rumours began to fly round our city that the French were supporting an attempt to negotiate by Mussolini.

'This dilatoriness by Great Britain was very disappointing, and I must say, a little frightening, too. If the big powers did not resist Hitler, there could be no hope for the little people in a Europe dominated by Germany.

'So when my friend told me that England had declared war, I felt a great relief. Believing that good must in the end triumph over wickedness, I felt confident that the British and their allies would win, and we should all be safe and happy once again.

'So I said to my friend, "It will be very bad for England before it is over, but whatever she suffers, it will be worth it to be the saviours of mankind. We shall have to do all we can to help, when it is over."

'It never occurred to me, nor to many Danes, I think, that before it was over, we and our country would be overrun and almost destroyed, before the British came and liberated us.'

In Stockholm, Sven Liberg was awakened by his mother and told the news.

He says, 'I was surprised to see that she was very upset. What did it matter to us Swedes what the big nations did? If they wanted to destroy one another, let them get on with it; it was no concern of ours, we could keep out of it like we had out of the last war. Besides, I knew a lot of Germans, and they were not so bad. They weren't fiends or monsters, but young men like me, who studied very hard, liked their beer and made love on Saturdays and Sundays and whenever else they could.

'So I said to my mother, "What are you so upset for? It's nothing to do with us." "You fool," she said. "Don't you realize that if the Germans win this war, they will make us their slaves, too?" "An old wife's tale," I replied. "Are you pro-Nazi?" she asked, her eyes shining with anger. I had never seen her quite so angry before, and though I was just past eighteen she scared me a little. "No," I mumbled, "I'm neutral." "That's as well," she said, "and if I hear one word to support the Germans from you, you will leave my house and take your Nazi ideas somewhere else, if you can find anyone to have you."

'I was so surprised by this outburst, that when she had gone downstairs again, I began to think seriously about it all. She was right, of course. If Germany defeated France and Britain, she would be master of all Europe, and that included Sweden. From that first day, I stopped being neutral, and I think, so did my country, for though diplomatically she maintained her policy of neutrality, secretly she did much to help the British, and, when they were occupied, our Norwegian and Danish brothers.'

Roger Makepeace had been to Oslo on business, and had arrived in Bergen on the Saturday evening to take the Sunday boat for Newcastle.

'I was still in bed, when there was a knock on my hotel bedroom door,' he recalls, 'and a young man put his head inside and somewhat embarrassed, excused himself. I asked him what he wanted.

'I am from the shipping company, sir,' he said. 'Because

of the international situation, the ship's sailing has been delayed. If war breaks out, the ship will not sail until the Norwegian colours have been painted on her sides, and that cannot be possibly done before tomorrow. We are warning all the passengers we can find.'

' "But I must be home tomorrow!" I exclaimed. "Are all the shipping lines cancelling their sailings?"

' "Yes, sir," I was told. "We are very sorry, but there is nothing we can do. If you will keep in touch with our office, we will give you what news we can."

'When he had gone, I got up and dressed and after drinking a cup of coffee I went out into the Bergen streets. There were quite a number of English holidaymakers all trying to get home, most of them, with that strange kind of don't-care attitude which the Englishman seems to think he must adopt when faced by difficulties, and which, in effect, makes his underlying anxiety all the more obvious.

'I could see that it would be no good laying siege to the shipping office until there was some definite news, so I went back to my hotel, and asked the manager if it would be possible for me to keep my room if the boat did not sail.

'He said, of course, and invited me into his office where he had his wireless tuned in to the B.B.C. Because of British summer time, we were on the same time as London, and there was still twenty minutes to go before quarter past eleven.

' "What do you think the news will be, Mr Makepeace?" the manager asked, handing me a glass of schnapps. "There can be only one kind of news," I said, "War!" "I think so, too, and I tell you that it will be best for all of us in the long run. That man will destroy us all if he is not stopped now. If it would help if Norway joined in, I would say, let us join." "You will be much more help to us out of it," I said. "Perhaps we shall not be able to stay out," he said. "But you are traditionally neutral," I reminded him. "Do you believe that anyone can be neutral with a modern war on your doorstep?" he asked.

'Before I could reply, the B.B.C. announcer was announcing the Prime Minister. I felt strangely anxious and relieved at the same time. During the past week in Oslo, a number of people had said to me that if it came to a showdown Chamberlain would not fight, and I had tried to tell them that Chamberlain was not England, and that if we did not like what he was doing it would not take us long to get rid of him, though I was sure that this time he would fight.

'When they played *God Save the King* at the end of the Prime Minister's broadcast, the manager of the hotel stood to attention at my side, and then lifted his glass, saying, "To a British victory—the only hope for the world." And I felt my eyes burning with tears of pride because people had such faith in us.'

As soon as I had telephoned the British Chargé d'Affaires in Tallinn and told him that I was taking my family home at the first possible moment, I telephoned to Madame Torvand-Tellmann and asked her to release me from my contract with her.

'Of course, Härra Seth, if you feel you must go,' she said. 'But why don't you wait a week or two. My husband says it will be all over in six weeks.'

I could not agree with General Torvand's appreciation of the situation, for what good would come of a negotiated peace, which was the only kind of peace which could come in six weeks?

I then telephoned the Rector of the University and asked him also to release me.

'Of course I understand,' he said. 'Come and see us before you go. We shall always have kind thoughts for you.'

My wife was in the kitchen preparing some food when I went in to tell her what I had done.

'How shall we go?' she asked.

'There will be only one way,' I said. 'From here to Helsinki, then from Finland to Stockholm, and from Stockholm to Bergen.'

'I see,' she said softly.

I went to her and took her in my arms, and held her close to me, and we clung to one another both wondering, I think, what would be the end of it all for us.

129

4

Act II - Afternoon

THE PRIME MINISTER had made his broadcast to the nation from No. 10 Downing Street. Immediately after it, he left for the House of Commons.

Reginald Parker, official chauffeur to five Prime Ministers, was turning his motor-car into Downing Street as the Alert sounded over London. Shortly after the wailing had died away, Mr Chamberlain came out of the house to the car.

Parker noted how drawn and tired the Prime Minister looked. Normally he had a greeting for his chauffeur; this morning he nodded and mumbled a pre-occupied time of day.

At eight minutes after noon, Chamberlain went to the despatch-box in a crowded House. The speech he made was a strange one. He spoke at length about himself and his past and present emotions; but he made not a single reference to Poland, the country on whose special behalf war had been declared.

While Duff Cooper and his little group had been meeting at Ronald Tree's house, Hugh Dalton and A. V. Alexander had gone to the house of Robert Vansittart, in Park Street, London, where Philip Noel Baker joined them.

Sir Robert was the Chief Diplomatic Adviser to the Government, and he had a curious tale to tell them. All the previous day he had waited in his office in the Foreign Office, waiting to be consulted if he should be needed, or at least courteously informed of what was going on.

No one had sent for him or telephoned him or communicated with him in any way. Nor had he been approached this morning.

While the four men chatted, a message came for Dalton

saying that the French Ambassador very much wished to see him before the House of Commons met. Dalton went at once to the Embassy, taking Alexander with him.

They were shown in to the Ambassador just as eleven o'clock was striking.

The Ambassador said he had asked them to call, because he was very worried by stories he had heard that some Members of Parliament were casting doubts on France's intention to declare war. He wished to reassure them that France would honour her pledges.

He went on to explain the difficulties in which France's vast mobilization plans involved her. The two Englishmen heard him out, and then stressing the danger that long delay would bring, especially in allowing the Germans to deploy their submarines, they left for a meeting of the Labour Party Executive at the House of Commons.

As Dalton was beginning his report of their meeting with the Ambassador, the sirens sounded and a policeman warned them to go to the shelters on the lowest floor, level with the terrace. So he was not able to tell his colleagues that France was definitely going to declare war.

What had happened in Paris was this. At first General Gamelin, the Commander-in-Chief of the French Army, had insisted that he must have until 4 a.m. at least on 4th September to bring mobilization to the degree of readiness which would enable the French Army to withstand an immediate assault should Hitler launch one, and this time had been inserted in the French ultimatum. However, during the morning M. Daladier, the Prime Minister, had argued once more with the General, and insisted that the time should be brought forward to five o'clock that afternoon.

M. Coulondre, the French Ambassador in Berlin, was on the point of setting out for the German Foreign Office to deliver the ultimatum, when Bonnet, the Foreign Minister, telephoned him to tell him of the new time. Another three minutes, and the Ambassador would not have been there.

Coulondre had asked Ribbentrop to receive him at noon, and as the Chaplain in the House of Commons was saying prayers, he was arriving in the Wilhelmstrasse.

131

Now, the Germans' new friends, the U.S.S.R., had appointed a new Ambassador in Berlin, and Hitler had set noon as the hour at which Comrade Alexander Shkvarzev was to present his Letters of Credence. Ribbentrop was at this ceremony, so M. Coulondre was received by Baron von Weizsacker, Secretary of State.

Coulondre asked Von Weizsacker if he were empowered to give a satisfactory answer to the French ultimatum, and was told that the Baron was not in a position to give a reply of any kind. The Ambassador interpreted this to mean that Germany would not give a satisfactory reply, and there upon attempted to hand the formal ultimatum to the Baron. But Von Weizsacker refused it, and asked Coulondre to be patient and wait for the Foreign Minister to arrive.

On several occasions in the past, Ribbentrop had treated Coulondre with scant courtesy and had kept him waiting for appointments. This time the Ambassador was kept waiting for half an hour, and was then taken to Hitler's Chancellery to the Foreign Minister.

Before M. Coulondre could state his business to Ribbentrop, though the German Foreign Minister knew why he was there, the former German Ambassador in London and one time darling of such aristocratic families as the Londonderrys, went into a long and false account of Mussolini's last-minute bid for peace, saying that Germany had been agreeable to the conference, and so, he understood, had France, but that the British had wrecked the plan.

Knowing that this was the last time that he would have to listen to Ribbentrop, Coulondre took a deep breath and interrupted him.

'Do these remarks of His Excellency mean that Germany's answer to the French Note of 1st September is negative?' he asked.

'*Ja!*' replied Ribbentrop.

Thereupon Coulondre handed over the ultimatum.

'If France attacks Germany she will be the aggressor,' Ribbentrop growled.

'History will be the judge of that,' the Ambassador replied, gave a slight bow, and withdrew.

In his office in Rome, the Italian Foreign Minister, Count Ciano, heard Chamberlain's declaration of war.

'I am not a military man,' he told himself, and later confided to his diary. 'I do not know how the war will develop, but one thing I know—it will develop and it will be long, uncertain and relentless. The participation of Great Britain makes this certain. England has made this declaration to Hitler. The war can end only with Hitler's elimination or the defeat of Britain.

As Chamberlain rose to speak in the House of Commons, the Donaldson Atlantic Lines passenger ship *Athenia*, was 296 miles from Liverpool, out in the broad waters of the Atlantic, bound for neutral ports.

At this very moment, too, one of the strangest incidents of the whole war was being enacted in London's West India Dock. The following account of it had been sent me by F. J. Allquist, who took part in it.

'There lay in the West India Dock, which was later to become a favourite target for Goering's bombers, a fine new German vessel of about 4,000 tons, called the M/V *Pamona*. She had arrived a few days before, unloaded a cargo of bananas, and then, being unable to pay her dock dues, had had a writ nailed to her mast, preventing her from leaving until the dues were paid.

'This non-payment of dues, and the fact that the vessel was a fine new one, makes the story all the more strange. For the past week the war-clouds had been so threatening that the outbreak of hostilities itself seemed inevitable. Indeed, as we know now, the German Government knew what it intended to do, and one would have thought that as shipping in wartime is more precious than gold, the Embassy in London would have got the *Pamona* out of her difficulties.

'But no one had lifted a finger to help, and here she was in the West India Dock, from eleven o'clock on 3rd September representing a most desirable Prize of War.

'Her master, whom I talked with several times—I was the foreman of M Shed—was an irascible man, and in a furious temper at his dilemma. So much so, that when on one occasion, in an attempt to pacify him I said, "Don't worry, there will be no war," he whirled round on me and wagging a finger right under my nose, growled, 'You vill see! You vill see!'"

'For the last day or two it had been rumoured in the docks that if war did break out, the *Pamona*'s master intended to start up his engines and ram the dock gates, which, if he succeeded, would be a severe act of sabotage. True or false, the authorities had decided to take no chances, and a contingent of the London Scottish had been detailed to mount guard at the foot of the gangway, with orders to prevent the ship from moving if she made any sign of doing so.

'Besides the London Scottish, an Auxiliary Fire Service squad had taken up their post about a mile away on the other side of the dock. They were volunteers, completely out of their depth among the docks and ships. Their equipment, too, was almost laughable in its simplicity and potential—a trailer pump hauled by a London taxi-cab.

'At eleven o'clock on the Sunday morning, I was standing talking to the A.F.S. men. An officer of the Port Staff was with us; he had listened in to the Prime Minister and had brought us the news that we were at war.

'Suddenly the sirens sounded. Now, as an infantryman in the last war, with a couple of years' experience on the Somme and at Vimy, I had a healthy respect for the Germans who had always seemed to me determined and dangerous fighters. So as I heard the sirens, I glanced across the dock wondering what the *Pamona*'s master would do.

'Almost immediately, from where she lay, a great billow of black smoke rose into that clear and sunny September sky from between her masts, which showed above the shed roofs.

'Involuntarily I shouted, "Christ! They've set her alight! She's on fire!"

'Knowing the area as I did, I visualized the dock sheds catching alight, and us in the centre of a sure target for the enemy bombers which I expected to arrive at any moment. So turning to the A.F.S. chap, no doubt somewhat crudely, I told him my fears. We were surely in the wrong place.

'Standing a few yards from the taxi was my car, and in answer to his question "How the hell do we get to it?" I shouted "Follow me," jumped in with the Port Staff officer beside me, and drove away.

'Around the dock basin we raced, the taxi bouncing behind with a rattling of fire gear, and presently turned on to the quay by the German vessel, whose whole midship upper structure was enveloped in thick black smoke.

'A startled and obviously puzzled guard still stood at the bottom of the gangway.

' "The ship's on fire!" I yelled, raced up the gangway and pulled up short on deck to look around. I could see no flame and could feel no heat. In seconds the A.F.S. man was beside me, complete with hose and nozzle at the ready, all connected to the hydrant, which his pal was ready to turn on.

'I had spent a life time on and around ships in the docks, and had once helped to quell a small fire aboard one, and it struck me that the fire here was in the engine-room, the steel ladder leading to which was only a few feet from where I stood. The ship was eerily quiet, ominously so, in fact, for a ship is rarely, if ever, absolutely quiet; there is always a heart beating below.

'But there was not a single sound. She seemed just like a dead ship, whose bilge pumps had ceased for ever their continuous rattle and squeak, whose dynamoes had stopped their humming, whose lights, which even in daylight shine through portholes in a live ship, had been doused for eternity.

'At any time one treads lightly over a dead ship, and as one does so, one invariably experiences an overwhelming sadness. By heaven, I had this feeling now.

'What would happen when we opened the steel door? Would flames dart out in angry attempts to devour us? Would the crew try to make a fight for it? What would happen?

'By this time, an officer of the shore guard had joined us. Turning to me, he asked if I knew my way about. Gingerly I opened the steel door. No flames nor any member

135

of the crew appeared, and gazing in all I could see was a black hole which smelled of oil and smoke.

'There is probably no part of a ship more awesome to a landlubber than the engine-room. Its narrow iron-slatted platforms cross twenty foot drops onto jagged engine tops, pistons and cranks and pipes. The steel narrow runged ladders are nearly perpendicular and you must climb down them into the reeking bowels of the ship. They are not too good to tackle when they are lighted, and now it was as black as Hitler's heart down there.

'On the platform there was no space in which two men might pass each other. A false step could heave you into space, to hurtle down onto the engines, to be broken or mangled.

'The officer said, "Has anyone got a torch?" Neither I nor the Port officer had, and the officer produced a pen-type one which is used for map-reading. Gingerly we crept along one platform and then the next, the officer leading.

'Presently he came to a door, and by the dim light of his so-called torch he slowly pulled it open. It was impossible to see what was inside, but a horrible stench of putrifying flesh rushed out at us. What had these murderous Jerries done? Who were the dead?

'Simultaneously with this discovery, there started a hissing and rumbling down below. I think it was the A.F.S. man who shouted, "They've put a bomb down there to blow her up." I froze, and my bowels went loose. It was going to be one hell of a job to get up and out in time.

'Suddenly the gloom lessened. Someone above had opened the engine-room skylights. Stumbling, we retraced our way back up the iron ladder. On the platform we met two figures barring our way. One I recognized as the German Captain, while behind him, holding on to his shoulder was a man I had known for many years—the Chief Inspector of the Dock Police. He must have heard the shout about the bomb.

'The Captain was protesting in voluble German, and the Inspector, who was never one to waste words, exclaimed, "Speak English, you bastard!" But to no avail; the flow of

German continued, until the Inspector's patience, like Hitler's, was exhausted.

' "Right," he said. "If we're going to blow up, we'll all blow up together."

'I fear that I was not a hundred per cent in favour of this. But we could not get past them, so we waited in silence, tense and fearful.

'As we stood there, presently up from the gloom came two of the German crew, who had obviously been preparing the trap below. They could not pass us either. I noticed that the army man was holding his revolver.

'And all the time we stood there, there was that hissing and rumbling, though nothing happened.

'Above us one of the Dockmaster's men was furiously turning the handle of a large wheel on the engine-room bulkhead.

'Of course, I thought, he's flooding the ship. Would the water reach the bomb before it went off? We waited in silence.

'The Inspector still held the Captain, who had at last obeyed his captors; the A.F.S. man held the hose nozzle; I could only hold my breath. Now the man turning the wheel spoke. "She's settling," he said. "I'm closing the water-tight doors." Then, I am sure to everyone's relief, the Inspector said, "Right, let's get to hell out of here."

'So we clambered out onto the beautifully sunlit deck. I must admit, and I believe I was not alone, that I had spent the most terrifying ten minutes of my life.

'But now came our turn to be surprised and in our surprise, to feel somewhat foolish.

'The Dockmaster had believed that the ship might make a run for it in order to ram another ship or the lock gates. To prevent this he had sent a powerful tug to moor itself against the vessel on the water side, and because the *Pamona* was so much larger than it, the tug was quite invisible to anyone on the quay. At the moment war was declared, the tug crew had stoked the boilers, and it was the copious clouds of smoke from the tug funnels which had enveloped the *Pamona*'s bridge, causing us to believe she was on fire.

137

'Between the short time of the tug raising steam, and nosing the vessel hard against the quayside, the alert crew of the tug noticed that the German ship was settling down in the water. A tugman raced on board, and it was he who was closing, not opening, the water-tight doors.

'The stench from the darkened room below, was not from corpses, but from decomposing meat stores, caused by a breakdown in the refrigeration plant when the ship's motors were stopped. This was also the cause of there being no lights aboard. The two Germans who had come up from below, had been opening the seacock and damaging parts of the engine. When we burst in they must have lain low, until persuaded to come up by the rising water, which was the noise we heard as it rushed in through the seacocks.

'Eventually the troops searched the ship, routed out the crew from their hiding places, and marched them off down the quay. At the head of the forlorn column were the Inspector and the Captain.

'As I leaned over the rails of the ship, I could hear the Captain protesting, and the Inspector say, "Never mind, Captain, I'm an old soldier. You know this kind of thing happens in a war." And the Captain, who really understood and spoke English perfectly, turned and smiled wanly at him.

'In time, the *Pamona* was cleaned, refitted and loaded, and a month later sailed under the British flag as the *Empire Merchant*. Sadly, she was torpedoed off the Irish coast on her first trip.

'In 1915, at the Battle of Loos, the London Scottish had a very tough scrap, and it was said, defended their cook-house with great valour. This was much publicized in the newspapers of the day who seemed to have forgotten that other troops were there as well. These other troops never let the London Scottish forget this, and would shout after them, "Who saved the dixies at Loos?" and in reply we would yell, "The London Scottish." Then the Navy sank the German cruiser *Emden*, and again we cried, "Who sank the *Emden*?" and once more supplied our own answer, "The London Scottish."

138

'Now, however, they could legitimately add to their battle honours the capture of the *Pamona*.

No earlier claim for the capture of a German ship in the Second World War has been recorded.

While the *Pamona* was thus falling victim to war, in Berlin the radio was announcing that Great Britain had declared war on Germany. Outside the Chancellory, their equivalent of No. 10 Downing Street, a small crowd of about three hundred had gathered in the bright sunshine.

They listened to the announcement in complete silence. A neutral has said that they appeared completely stunned by it. How could their Leader have led them into war after all he had said about not wanting war?

Goebbels, the Minister for Public Enlightenment, had got quickly off the mark. On his instructions the newspapers had prepared an emergency issue, which appeared on the streets shortly after noon, and were given away.

The *Deutsche Allgemeine Zeitung*, typical of the rest, carried the headlines:

BRITISH ULTIMATUM REJECTED
ENGLAND DECLARES A STATE OF WAR WITH GERMANY
BRITISH NOTE DEMANDS WITHDRAWAL OF OUR
TROOPS IN EAST
FÜHRER LEAVING FOR FRONT TODAY
GERMAN MEMORANDUM PROVES ENGLAND'S GUILT

This last was interesting, but only as a crude attempt by the German leaders to free themselves of their guilt in the eyes of their own people. Ribbentrop had taken exactly this line when Sir Nevile Henderson, whom he had sent for, arrived to receive the German reply.

Ribbentrop told the Ambassador that he could inform his Government that the German Government refused to receive, let alone comply with, their ultimatum. He then handed Henderson a memorandum—that quoted in the newspapers —which repeated all the old German lies, stated that Germany had accepted Mussolini's efforts to call a conference, which had been frustrated by Britain's refusal to join such a conference (Germany had not, in fact, agreed) and concluded by accusing Britain of 'preaching the destruction and extermination of the German people.'

Sir Nevile read the memorandum through quickly and remarked, 'History will judge where the blame really lies.'

'History has already proved the facts,' Ribbentrop replied with unconscious irony.

A few minutes after eleven o'clock, the Head of the Treaty Department in the British Foreign Office, called at the German Embassy in London and was received by the German Chargé d'Affaires. He handed the Chargé Britain's formal declaration of war and withdrew.

He had not yet returned to the Foreign Office, when the operator in the switchboard there, plugged in to receive a telephone call.

Jack McLoughlin was the operator, and he recalls, 'I was in the telecommunications department of the G.P.O. at the time. I had been working at the Air Ministry, but on the morning of 3rd September, owing to the sudden illness of our staff at the Foreign Office, two of us were sent across to replace them.

'There was some confusion: among other things there were no plans or diagrams of the new telephone switchboard which had been installed in the shelter.

'After the siren went off, we all went to the shelter, and almost immediately a call came through on the emergency switchboard. It was from the German Embassy, and the girls got a bit flustered. They knew that Lord Halifax was in the building, but the various private wires had not been marked. We could only suggest that they try all the lines until they got the right one.

'By the time they got through, Lord Halifax had left. They explained this to the Embassy, and asked if the Permanent Under-Secretary of State would do or anybody else.

'Yes, of course, they were told. They merely wanted to be sure that their old black dog, (which used to be quite a landmark sitting on the Embassy steps) would be looked after, as they could not take him to Germany with them.

'When Lord Halifax arrived, somebody told him about the incident, and tired and weary though he was, he immediately gave instructions to have the dog attended to. This human touch at the beginning of the world's greatest conflict will always remain vividly with me.'

The meeting of Parliament on a Sunday was an extraordinary event in the political life of England. There had been only two other Sunday meetings in the past two hundred years, and both of them had been made necessary under the old law by which the death of the Sovereign automatically dissolved Parliament. George II and George III had both died on a Saturday.

This session on 3rd September, 1939, lasted from noon until 12.47 p.m., then the House went into Committee to consider four Bills.

The first of these was the National Service (Armed Forces) Bill, and as the House began to debate it, a solemn ceremony was being enacted in Eltham, South-east London.

The officers of the 54th (City of London) Heavy Anti-Aircraft Regiment Artillery, Territorial Army, had requisitioned a house in Eltham to act as local H.Q. and mess.

When luncheon had finished, the Commanding Officer, Lieutenant-Colonel J. W. Perring R.A. (T.A.), rose and addressed his officers in the following words, so far as Colonel Eustace Shipman T.D., then the junior of two medical officers attached to the Regiment, can remember.

'Gentlemen,' said Colonel Perring, 'we are now proud members of the Regular Army, for on the outbreak of war, the Territorial Army ceases to exist. It becomes our duty, therefore, to remove the insignia which distinguishes us Territorials from our professional brethren. Therefore, gentlemen, you will join with me in removing the offending insignia in accordance with Regulations.'

So saying, he crossed his arms, seized the little metal 'Ts' which Territorial officers wore on their epaulettes, and wrenched them out of the cloth, leaving two jagged tears. All his officers followed suit.

The small pieces of brass were placed in a bowl which was passed round the table. Later, they were melted down and cast into a large 'T' which was inscribed with the names of all present.

141

As will be recalled, on the Friday evening Mr Chamberlain had invited Winston Churchill to become a member of the small War Cabinet he intended to set up. As Churchill had understood it, he was to be a Minister Without Portefolio, and though he would have preferred a Department he had decided to accept.

All day Saturday he had waited for confirmation to come from the Prime Minister, but had received no word, and at one time had considered changing his mind about accepting. In a somewhat angry mood, just before midnight on the Saturday, he had written and sent to Chamberlain a letter asking the Prime Minister to see him before the session opened in the House on Sunday.

On his arrival at the House, he found a note from Chamberlain asking him to call on him as soon as the debate died down. Though this was something, it was not entirely satisfactory from Churchill's point of view. He would have liked to have said some words in the debate, but because he considered himself to be a member of the Government, he refrained from doing so, and thus his name is missing from the record on the only Parliamentary event of importance in over thirty years.

When the Prime Minister withdrew from the chamber, Churchill followed him to his room, and there Chamberlain explained that since they had last met on Friday, he had had second thoughts about the War Cabinet. He now intended to expand it, to take in the Service Ministers, and since Lord Stanhope, the present First Lord of the Admiralty, had consented to become Lord President of the Council, Chamberlain was able to offer Churchill this Office.

Churchill had held this post for a time in the First World War, and he was delighted at the prospect of filling it again. So he accepted and at once sent a note to the Admiralty— Chamberlain had told him that if he accepted the appointment was effective from that moment—saying that he would arrive to take charge at six o'clock.

On receiving this news, the Board of Admiralty caused a signal to be despatched to every ship and British naval establishment throughout the world: 'Winston is back!'

One of the officers to receive this signal was Lieutenant-Commander Lord Mountbatten. He had been appointed a few days earlier to the command of H.M.S. *Kelly*, and he was at sea working up the ship which had been recently built and newly commissioned.

Another was Admiral Sir A. B. Cunningham. He was on the fore turret of H.M.S. *Malaya* in Alexandria harbour watching the 1st Battle Squadron's Regatta.

Speaking of his reactions to the earlier news that England was at war, Admiral of the Fleet Lord Cunningham of Hyndhope says, 'One's thoughts at such a moment are somewhat chaotic, but I remember distinctly casting over in my mind the preparations we had made for this event and finding that there seemed to be nothing more to do. Our plans were fully up to date.

'I also thought that the highly efficient Mediterranean Fleet would now start to melt away as the Italians would wait to see how the cat would jump—and so indeed it happened.'

As Churchill left Chamberlain's room, England began to sit down to the Sunday roast; soon to be remembered as a luxury, a status-symbol of better times. In a camp on a ridge overlooking Mellor in Cheshire, it was the quietest and most sombre meal in which the campers had participated since they had assembled.

Ironically, it was called a Peace Camp. It had been organized by the local Refugee Committee and members of the Labour League of Youth. Among the latter present this Sunday and at this midday meal was Mrs Joyce Cooper, who describes the scene.

'Most of the refugees were from Austria and Germany. There was Oscar, an intense Austrian Jewish boy, who was learning French because he believed the revolution would start there. He trembled every time we sang *The Red Flag*, because it was also the tune used for the *Horst Wessel*, the Nazi Party song.

'There were two middle-aged German Jews with mouthfuls of gold teeth replacing those knocked out in Buchenwald, from which awful place miraculously and unaccountably they had been released.

143

'There was Mrs Heinz Eisler, with her son, waiting to join her composer husband in the U.S.A. And there was Fritz.

'Fritz was a German Jew of seventeen. His wealthy father had sent him to England, but one had the impression of a reluctant refugee, for he believed fervently in the Nazi doctrine of "Might is Right."

'There were many others too, sitting at the tables in the mess tent. Before, these occasions had been noisy and jolly affairs for most, but this Sunday lunch eyes were downcast, tongues were silent, lips could not smile.

'That England and Germany had embarked on war was serious enough, but it hit much nearer home than a fight between countries. For since eleven o'clock we, who for the past week had been steadily forging links of friendship, had become, officially, enemies, and none of us quite knew how to cope with the situation.

'Incidentally, all those I have named were later interned —all of them except Fritz!'

If these Austrians and Germans were safe, though in an enemy country, there were countless millions of their fellow-countrymen at home who saw themselves in the direst peril.

'When I heard over our radio that England had declared war on Germany,' says Frau Anni Straus of Frankfort-am-Main, 'I just broke down and wept. I had three sons all in the army, and I knew that fighting England would not be the same thing as going gaily into a friendly Austria or fighting a weak Poland. England was a stubborn and courageous country. She would fight until she had won or until Germany had completely wiped her out, and for what reason?

'By this time many of us, who had welcomed the order and prosperity compared with the chaos and starvation and misery which we had suffered under the Weimar Republic, which the Nazi Party had managed to provide, had lost all sympathy with their warlike aims. They talked of Lebensraum and of *One Folk, One Reich*. But we had all the room we needed, and the Germans who lived in other countries

144

were quite happy until these devils came along and told them they were unhappy. There was no need to fight."

'Well, this would be the end of them, and for that one felt relieved by the news. Someone had succeeded where we had failed, and had had the courage to stand up to them. But before the end came what should we—and not only us but English mothers and French mothers—suffer, and our husbands and our sons.

'I got down on my knees and prayed for the first time for many years. I prayed, "Oh God, help us to support the suffering and make the end worth it all!" Today, I think He must have heard my prayers, though I lost two of my sons.'

Franz Bütt was a boy of sixteen, a member of the Hitler Youth. 'I was at a meeting when we were told that England had declared war on Germany. Our leader made a long speech, saying that now more than ever we must dedicate our lives to our Führer and our Fatherland, that we must have no fear of the outcome, that victory always favoured the just.

'I remember feeling so proud, and I actually saw visions of how I would perform great deeds for the beloved Führer and for Germany. But within little more than a year, all these dreams had vanished. I was in the Army serving in Yugoslavia, and I had seen hundreds of men, women and children driven on to the ice of a river, and I had heard the ice crack under them and their screams as the water closed over their heads, and in that moment known that such bestial cruelty was doomed to be overcome in the end.

'I am writing to you, sir, hoping that you will print what I have said, so that it may be a warning. There is no more easy target for corruption by wicked men than youth, for I tell you, there were many of my friends who drove those women and children on to the ice, and were happy to do it. I was lucky, because at the back of me there were good parents and a good home, whom, though I despised them for their apparent weakness at the time, nevertheless inculcated into me a fundamental decency. But there were many from homes like mine, who had all the decency knocked out of them and only too late saw their error.'

Walter Schmidt was in Bremen on this day, and heard the news on board the merchant ship on which he served.

'This is what I had feared,' he says. 'This was what I had hoped would never happen. But now that it had happened, in my heart I felt glad in a sad way. We often called at English ports, and once I had had an English girl-friend whom I nearly married. I could not believe that she and I were now enemies. If only . . . But what's the use of "if onlys"?'

Gunter Altman was a small shop-keeper in a small village outside Munster. 'I had fought as a young boy in the first European war, and I did not want to fight in another, nor did I want my sons and my daughters to know the suffering which war, whether you are the victor or the vanquished, inevitably brings, despite the fact that all of them had grown away from their mother and me during the last years as the Nazis gained more and more control of their young minds.

'I was serving in my little shop when the news came that England had declared war on Germany. There were two or three women and one man waiting to be served. The women, who had been serious when they came in, fell silent as the radio gave the news and they all turned pale. One of them, a young woman with a husband already with the army, began to weep, and as one of the older women went to comfort her, the man, who was a stranger to us, growled, "Why do you weep? This is the best thing that could happen. They've fed us on lies all these years, and these lies that we have just heard are the biggest of them all. When this is all over we shall be able to get back to the truth. You'll see."

'He then asked me for a few grammes of sausage and some fat, and went out. I did not speak to him, except to tell him how much he owed me, for the simple reason I was too surprised that anyone should have the courage to say what he thought to strangers. The women were affected as I was, too, except the young woman, who, through her tears, muttered "Communist".

'But whether he was a Communist or not, I knew at once that he had spoken the truth. For all these years we had lost

146

all courage to the extent that we would not recognize lies and were ready to accept them as the truth. Now we were going to reap the harvest of our cowardice. I prayed that what we should suffer would be a refining fire. I think it has been.'

In Austria, in the little town of Salzburg, famous for all time as the birthplace of Mozart, Frieda Vogl heard the news in her little room.

'I was shocked,' she writes, 'and the hatred which I had had for the Germans ever since they had taken over our country bubbled over. England had declared war, and that meant a long struggle, for the English are a proud and obstinate race, who, protected by their great moat, could defy any power. Because of the Anschluss, Austria was also at war, whether we Austrians wanted to be or not—and I do not believe that one of us did—and all one could hope for was that when it was over we should be free once more. From that moment, I made up my mind that I would work for my country's freedom. When it came to the point, there was not much I could do, but the little I did, and I am glad I did it.'

The Italian people did not want war. Mussolini knew it, but he knew too, what the ordinary man-in-the-street did not know—that Italy was completely unprepared for war.

'I was not sorry,' writes Enrico Vivaldo of Milan, 'when I heard that England had got back her courage and had challenged Hitler to battle. At the same time, however, I was very much afraid of what Mussolini would do. I am sure that I was only one of millions who felt this way: that if he declared war in support of his German buddy, our country would soon be locked in the most disastrous convulsions which had ever overtaken it since the Risorgimento; and this we were not ready to withstand, for we were all so weary. But as I thought more about it, it suddenly occurred to me: perhaps this can be our salvation after all. For the first time in years, I went into a church and prayed that it would be so.'

Signora Eurosina Patuzzo was the mother of five children under the age of eleven. 'As it was Sunday we had decided

147

to go to the beach at Ostia—we were living in Rome, as we are now, though in a different house—and after Mass we took the bus.

'People on the bus were all talking excitedly about what was going to happen. Some argued that England would not fight because Chamberlain was too weak, and we had heard that the Duce was trying to get them all to a conference which would solve all the problems which still existed. Others reminded these people that the English people still had the power to get rid of their Government if they did not like it (this was a very outspoken thing to say, because of its implications) and one man said that his cousin had recently been to England, and there was a very different spirit there now, from what there had been at the time of Munich. But whether we were on one side of the argument or the other, all of us hoped that our Duce would keep us out of war.

'There were quite a lot of people on the beach, but what struck me most was that except for the shouts and laughs of the children, there was only a low murmur of conversation instead of the happy cries that usually made an excursion to the beach so good.

'As far as I can remember, it was in the early afternoon that the news that England had declared war reached the beach. It spread among the people, from mouth to mouth, like a fire in a forest. Soon some people began to pack up and go home, and I felt that I must join them. This time there was hardly any conversation at all. The main thought that was in everybody's mind I am sure, was what I was thinking: What would the Duce do? For the sake of my children, I prayed that he would find a way to keep Italy at peace.'

While Signora Patuzzo was wondering what the Duce would do, Hugh Dalton, the Socialist politician, was in the Lobby of the House of Commons speaking to the Polish Ambassador, Count Edward Raczynski. At 2 a.m. Dalton had telephoned Raczynski the news that England was presenting an ultimatum to Germany that morning, and the Ambassador was now telling him that he himself had then telephoned the news to his colleagues in Paris, Ambassador Lukasiewicz who had said that it seemed too good to be true.

As Raczynski left him, Dalton caught sight of Ivan Maisky, the Russian Ambassador in London, probably of all the Soviet representatives to serve in London, the most respected and liked.

Maisky looked tense and unhappy, Dalton noted as he walked over to him. The sudden Pact signed between Ribbentrop and the Russian Foreign Minister, had had the effect of isolating Maisky from many of his English friends.

Going up to him, Dalton greeted him and said, 'Your Government has greatly disconcerted us, but I hope that some of us will still keep in touch with you from time to time.'

Maisky replied, 'I hope so, too. And don't believe everything you read about our pact with Germany. We are neutral now, but all our future actions will be guided by self-interest, not by sentiment.'

In a train going from Peterborough to Birmingham, the cast of the show called *Runaway Love* had heard the news of the declaration of war on a portable radio, which they had kept tuned in so as to keep in touch with developments.

Now there came an announcement that all theatres, cinemas, race meetings and concerts were to be discontinued. The artistes looked at one another and began to wonder what was to become of them.

The senior member, Barry Lupino, of the famous theatrical family, blew his nose loudly and deliberately replaced his handkerchief, while he made sure that he had the attention of the others in the compartment.

'Judging from my experience in the last war,' he said, 'I am going to urge that all of us keep together. I think you will find that when things have shaken down, they'll ask the theatres to open again—morale and all that, you know.'

Irene Ashton, who appeared in the show as a pianist with Bill Mayerl, says, 'He proved right. A week or two later *Runaway Love* opened at the Saville Theatre in London and ran quite a long time. During the run we noticed quite a strange thing: good news rather tended to keep the seats unoccupied, bad news filled the theatre.'

In the German naval base at Wilhelmshaven, the German U-boat chief, Commodore Doenitz, was in conference with his staff. Presently he was interrupted by a messenger who held out to him a teleprinted note marked *Immediate*.

'The following,' he read, 'is a signal which has been sent to all British warships and merchant ships. Signal reads "Total Germany".'

He read out the message to his staff and told his second in command to draft the necessary signals to all U-boat commanders.

While this was being done, the passengers on board the Donaldson Atlantic liner *Athenia*, were settling down after lunch to while away the afternoon, many of them going up on deck to enjoy the sunshine, quite ignorant of the fact that the U-30's commander was steaming to take up position in the operational area allocated to him, and that the *Athenia*'s course was to take her through this area.

Hitler had listened to his wooden-headed Foreign Minister and had taken his advice, because that was what he wanted to hear. Great Britain will *not* go to war, Ribbentrop had assured him.

Now Ribbentrop had been proved wrong. Great Britain had declared war on Germany; France would do so in a few hours. If Hitler ever wondered why he had listened to Ribbentrop, short of withdrawing from Poland immediately there was nothing he could do to change the situation. Withdrawal from Poland was unthinkable, therefore war with Britain and France was inevitable.

Roundabout two o'clock, the Führer sat down at his desk in the Reichs Chancellery in Berlin, and for a few minutes scribbled a note or two on a pad. Presently he rang for his confidential secretary-stenographer, and dictated.

SUPREME COMMANDER OF THE ARMED FORCES
MOST SECRET

Berlin, 3rd September, 1939
Directive No. 2 for the Conduct of the War

In the Directive which followed, Hitler told his Generals that although England and France had declared war on Germany, the German war objective for the time being remained the speedy and victorious conclusion of the struggle with Poland.

Germany would not open hostilities in the West until Britain and France made the first move, with this exception —offensive naval operations against the British could begin at once.

Even the Luftwaffe was not to attack British objectives unless the Royal Air Force bombed Germany; and then only if the chances of success were favourable.

The whole German industrial potential was to be placed forthwith on a war footing.

Directive No. 2 was flashed to all the German leaders, and among its recipients was Commodore Doenitz. Immediately on receiving it, Doenitz signalled all his operational U-boats the information that Germany was at war with England and France, and ordered them to open attack at once on all British naval units and armed merchantmen in accordance with German Naval Prize Regulations.

The signal stated specifically, 'Do not wait until attacked.'

This signal was handed to the commander of the U-30, Oberleutnant Fritz Julius Lemp at about 4 p.m. G.M.T. He was already in his operational area—a rectangle two hundred by one hundred and eighty miles, bounded by 57°N and 19°W. He began to patrol on the surface.

The *Athenia*, unknown to Lemp and ignorant of the U-boat's presence ahead, was steaming at a steady fifteen knots straight for this area, and was only about seventy-five miles away.

As Hitler was dictating his Directive No. 2 Mrs Sydney Beale was sitting in the village hall at Chidham, near Chichester, waiting for evacuee children to arrive.

On 17th September, she began to keep a war diary, and has sent me the following extracts from it.

'I kept a diary in the 1914-18 war, and I now take it up again. I find I wrote on 10th August, 1914, "When we are settled down again to our quiet smoothgoing lives, this time of unending suspense will have been the most interesting, though the most terrible of our lives."

'Looking back now on the years from 1918 to now (1939) I think that that was so, up to about a year ago. All this last year of suspense has again been terrible, and we have, except for the actual fighting of armies, been at war.

The crisis of last September left us feeling that we could not go on living under such strain, and stand by whilst Germany marched into any more countries. Early this year, everything was planned for evacuating women and children from the big towns in case of war.

'We all attended First Aid and Gas Lectures, etc., last winter. I have had to be the Women's Voluntary Services representative for this parish. Life has been like living on the edge of a precipice. Then two weeks ago today, on the 3rd September, we heard Chamberlain's broken voice on the wireless, telling us that we were at war. All this last two weeks I had meant to write a diary, but have lost count of days and time. The general impression is of a time of tremendous effort. Compared with 1914, the great differences are that we were prepared, and almost everyone quietly stepped into their job, without feverishly looking about to find out what they could or should do. Then getting the wireless news is another great difference, comforting yet upsetting, too.

'We were all four, Sydney (Major Beale), Joan (a student at the Royal Veterinary College) and Martin (a Harrow boy) ready to go to Torquay on 27th August for the National Dinghy Championships, but things looked so uncertain that Sydney and I both had to be here in connection with the evacuation, if things should happen. So we sent the children on, trailing their dinghy behind the car.

'By Thursday, 31st August, I found that my W.V.S. helpers did not at all want me to go, so Sydney started by train for Torquay. Five minutes after he left, we got a message to stand by to receive evacuees. I got a phone message through and stopped him at Southampton and he returned at once.

'On Friday we and the billeting officer and other helpers were at the village hall wondering what type of children or

152

mothers and babies we should get. We had been told to wait there with the District Nurse and other helpers. The Women's Institute, of which I, as President, prepared tea. Rations for each child had arrived from London over night, also seventeen blankets.

'Eventually a bus-load arrived from Tooting district, all nice-looking big girls, also two masters with several children from a large mixed school. We got them placed in billets previously canvassed for. Then for two more days we sat in the village hall waiting, but no more came.

'It was on Sunday, whilst we were waiting at the hall, that we heard we were at war. About half an hour or so after Chamberlain's speech, we had our first air-raid warning, and that morning the telephone was installed in the hall, because it was the ambulance and A.R.P. headquarters as well. The drivers and wardens all turned up. It was a false warning, but compare that with one hour after the 1914 war started. The strong emotions of the last war—which makes one realize a good deal of what it all means to go through—is perhaps rather difficult for a second time in an adult life? But everything is so much more prepared and organized and quietly accepted, with less heroic feelings perhaps.'

How well prepared and organized seemed a matter of individual experience, for while Mrs Beale was thinking these thoughts in Chidham village hall, Miss Helen Dedman, the headmistress of a junior mixed and infants school in East London, whom we have previously met, was wandering about Bury St Edmunds in Suffolk trying to find pupils who were still 'lost'.

They had become lost like this.

On arrival at Bury St Edmunds, the billeting officials and their helpers had been on the point of going home, and there had been one or two difficulties in getting them all placed. When at last all the children had been found homes, Miss Dedman then found that there had been quite a serious oversight.

She writes: 'Each child was to have been given a post-card on which was written the new address. They were to be

153

sent at once to parents, so that they should not worry too much. I now discovered that these cards had not been distributed. But these cards were of the utmost importance if the peace of mind of parents were not to be too greatly overtaxed; after all, parting with one's children, entrusting them to the hands of strangers, is no light thing for a father or a mother.

'I gave the Chief Billeting Officer one of my nominal rolls, and asked if I might be supplied with the children's addresses so that I could let the parents know their whereabouts, but was told that was impossible. I then offered to make a list myself if I might have access to the billeting officers' books. This certainly could not be allowed.

'When all the children were gone, the teachers were given billets. I asked for a billet for one, and my sister, who was staying a few days to see us settled in, did the same. We did not realize it at the time, but, quite naturally, those who had offered to receive one only, were the folks who lived in the tiniest cottages.

'A kind lady took me and my sister by car to the address given to my sister. It was a small house with front door and one window down and one window upstairs. A shaky old man came to the door and said, "Yes, we did say we would take one child, but my old woman was taken to the asylum last week, and I couldn't have one now, especially a lady."

'We then went on to my address. Here a farm labourer and his wife said, looking most alarmed, "Oh, we couldn't possibly take a teacher!" I expected to be taken back to the billeting station, but our nice driver said she knew someone who would take us for the night.

'We were very warmly received and were offered a bath. It was now after nine o'clock, and after such a hot and trying day, we must have looked as though that was what we most needed, as indeed it was. I shall never forget the luxury of that bath. We were then given a meal, the first since breakfast in our own homes, and went to bed.

Our bedroom was an attic, heated all day by the sun, and now hermetically sealed by the black-out. The beds were new iron single ones, made up with new sheets which rustled

154

so that, after I had tossed and turned for a time, my sister asked, "Are you sleeping on brown paper?"

'Next day we found that there was another attic in which there were three exactly similar beds, for our two hostesses were prepared to receive five children. They were anxious that I should stay there and find four children to complete the party, but it was on the outskirts of the town, and having thanked them for their hospitality, we returned to the billeting station to ask for a billet nearer the centre. One of the billeting officers offered to take me in, and I found a home where I was as happy and comfortable for the next four years as war conditions allowed.

'But until I had found all my children, I could have no peace of mind. So that day I wandered about Bury hoping to meet some of them who would also be able to tell me where friends were. The first child I met now lived at No. 1 the Ruins, The Churchyard (really an aristocratic habitation, I discovered later) and I wondered what impression her parents would get from such an address.

'I asked the next, a little girl of six, whether she was happy in her new home. "Yes, thank you," she said, "as happy as a sand-bag."

'I was still at it on Sunday morning, when war was declared, and not until late that evening had I found them all and sent off the cards to parents.'

J. F. L. Gates, a schoolmaster, also found things to irritate him on this day.

'With other members of the staff,' he says, 'I arrived at school early on the Sunday morning to complete the lists of names of children to be evacuated if war should break out. We were in an area of potential but not actual danger, and for this reason had not had to make preparations unless things began to look really serious.

'As with others at the time, we were clinging to the last bit of optimism and though writing names, home addresses and next-of-kin, we were hoping that such lists would never be needed and that evacuation for us would be unnecessary.

'The headmaster brought his portable wireless set with him, and was sitting in his room waiting for the Prime Minister's speech. In my classroom I was busily writing, concentrating on getting the list absolutely accurate, when suddenly the door opened and the headmaster announced, "It's war!" I was ruling a line at that moment and in my agitation the ruler slipped and the line went diagonally across the page to register permanently my nervous reaction.

'Shortly afterwards the sirens sounded, and we all trooped into the playground to gaze skywards. Not for long, though, for an officious and conscientious air-raid warden emerged from his shelter in a corner of the playground and marched us into the school building, there to stand in the corridor gazing at each other—men teachers on one side, women teachers on the other!

'The All Clear released us from this preposterous situation and I made my way home to be greeted by my sister and our next-door neighbour, who had been weeping over the fence, because Poor Jack was in that terrible building and was sure to be killed.'

But on the other side, Miss F. R. Levy paints a picture which well illustrates the devotion to service which those on the receiving end of the evacuation, one of the greatest population movements ever experienced in this country, gave unstintingly.

'I was W.V.S. Centre Leader for Leatherhead, Surrey,' she writes, 'which was a Reception Area for four thousand evacuees, and had had very little time to sleep from the previous Wednesday.

'I remember someone on the Sunday morning beseeching me to have some breakfast, but we had too many people streaming in to ask questions and the telephones were all going, so that one could not leave the Centre. Nor was there a convenient hotel or café to which one might have gone, in any case.

'Eventually, I said that we really ought to get a bit of a break while Chamberlain was broadcasting, and so someone nobly went home and came back with tea, toast and a fried egg and bacon, and produced it, looking very appetizing, at exactly eleven o'clock.

'I cleared the middle of my table and started on it, and

at the precise moment when I took the first mouthful, a homesick girl of eight, who had been bothering me to send her back to London, came in, leant over me and fainted, and her hair, done up in long plaits, fell into the bacon and egg.

'Of course by the time she and I had been cleaned up, I had neither appetite nor space for eating, because the queue of visitors engulfed us again. My father, who was over seventy, and all sorts of people came along to try to solve problems and lessen the numbers of inquirers we each had to deal with. The worst of it was that the two helpers who had undertaken to deal with (a) billeting and (b) transport, had gone far away on holiday, and did not get back till about the 8th September.'

The sight of the patient queues of children waiting for trains that were to take them away from home and parents' love, moved many to volunteer their services at once. One such was Miss Frances Miller, who recalls, 'I was in London on the Friday taking my sister across to Victoria Station, and while we were there waiting for her train the newspapers came out with their headlines telling of Germany's attack on Poland. I was worried, because I was sure that this meant war for us as well.

'Then going home I saw a crowd of children with their numbers on labels tied to the coats waiting for the trains to take them to the Midland towns to which they were being evacuated. I knew then that I must do something to help. All day Saturday I thought it all over, wondering what I could do for the best.

'After Mr Chamberlain's broadcast on the Sunday, I made up my mind. I put on my hat and coat and went out and found the nearest recruiting office, and volunteered for the A.T.S. This, I thought, was the best way I could help to get those little children back to their homes and loved ones.'

Doing something was what most people wanted to be at more than anything else, and in most cases there was something which could be done.

Mrs Marie Ainsworth, who now lives in Victoria, Australia, writes, 'I was only just old enough *not* to be evacuated, so that fateful day found me in a damp steamy cellar in Manchester, working tirelessly at a mountain of washing which had to be dried and mended and packed up and sent away early next morning with its seven young owners.

'There I was, endlessly putting name tags on rubber boots and sandshoes; helping the overworked mother make hasty meals for the little ones as we worked and worked. I was longing for excitement, and wondering what my lucky brother was doing on his holidays in the south.

'Comparing notes later, I found out that he and his friend were up on the Sussex Downs at the Devil's Elbow, watching and listening for our planes' first sorties, while his friend's brother, now my husband but not then known, was serving aboard H.M.S. *Wyvern*, already on active monœuvres, chasing the enemy a few miles south and east in the English Channel.

'Excitement indeed! Eighteen hours approximately of solid humdrum work for me; but I would do it again and again. Now I have nine children of my own!'

Miss E. T. Barlow also kept a diary, in which she recorded, 'The most unSunday Sunday we have ever had. There was a thunder storm gathering when I went to bed, and it got very bad and went on till about 2 a.m. I got up a bit later than usual and got on with what had to be done in a leisurely fashion, and at ten o'clock Mary from London walked in.

'I was absolutely astonished and managed to think of a lot of possibilities before she said that she had brought down their valuables to find out if we could deposit them in our bank as theirs in London is quite full. She said her mother was getting all worked up and saying that God has forsaken us since this has come, and her sister is a bit nervy.

'She said, too, that London looked just as usual; there were still swarms of children about in their district, but she had seen little groups collecting with their parents evidently preparing for evacuation. She went back by the one fifty-five; practically the normal service is running.

'She came down with me to see the eleven-forty-five in, but very few, barely twenty, came by it. One was a mother with twins, one fourteen days and the other twelve days old,

158

and the granny. Dr A. took special care of them, and the babies delighted everyone. They were sent to Donnington.

'Mr Geils and I had just seen them settled in the car that was to take them when we saw a lot of the helpers tearing off down the street. Something was said about an air-raid warning, but we had not heard anything. However, there seemed a general idea that there was one and as there was nothing further to do I ran off home as fast as I could . . .

'The warning was rather odd; no sirens were sounded but there really was some sort of message about an impending air-raid sent to the station-master. T. says that all England is to be warned if there is a raid anywhere, so we are likely to get used to what Mr Luxford calls Mournful Mary.

'The trains in the afternoon both came down empty; it seemed rather ominous to me; the great length of the train slid in past all our waiting figures, and carriage after carriage as it passed was blank. I could not help wondering to what Mary was going back.

'Mrs B. was in in the evening; she thinks there is going to be a terrible muddle tomorrow about the billets; a train of 500 is expected at 5 a.m. She has been having extra-large meals prepared these last few days in case the children come, and is now going to have a mother and four children instead of six unaccompanied children.

'She wants to get a spade and pail tomorrow, and is also so anxious to grow food that she has sent to Suttons for as much spinach seed as they can send. I hope it won't arrive in a crate.

'How odd it all is. I turned up one of the pamphlets just now to refer to a point in connection with gas-masks and as I noted the title, *If War Comes*, and remembered how I felt about it when it was still *If*, it seemed almost incredible that that *If* must now be cancelled.'

How odd it all was indeed!

H. King worked on an R.A.F. station, and he had to report for duty on this day, and as he was on his way, the sirens sounded.

He recalls, 'About a quarter of a mile from the station

there was a deep dip in the road lined with a small spinney, an orchard and deep ditches. There I and the friend who was giving me a lift, were stopped by an N.C.O. and Service Policeman, who said, "You can't go into the station. Orders are dispersal and everybody take cover."

'At that moment, gazing round I saw some dozens of faces suddenly pop up all around us, in the long grass and bushes. My friend was allowed to go on, as he was a policeman, but I was made to disembark. I made for rough ground near a pool to find it was already over-crowded with airmen taking cover. I stood behind a stout tree alongside the road.

'Here the tempo was rising for many N.C.O.s were urging the airmen to hurry from their hutments to take cover across the road in bushes, and whistles were blown short and sharp with orders to double up there.

'After what seemed like a very long time, I saw some planes coming over the station, very large and flying low. This is it, I thought. They passed over the station—no bombs dropped—and headed straight for us it seemed. Did they know where we were?

'I feared the slaughter that must follow for there were over a thousand airmen in the vicinity. But they roared overhead to cries of "They're ours! They're ours!" They were too. But what would have happened if they had not been, I've always wondered?'

Air Vice-Marshal W. M. Yool was having quite a different experience at this time. He was a member of a mission to the French Air Force Headquarters, which had spent the previous week at Versailles getting to know their opposite numbers.

Before leaving England they had been told that if war broke out they would be moved into headquarters at St Jean les Deux Jumeaux, on the Marne, where they would find a direct telephone line to the Air Ministry in London.

Early on the Sunday morning they had received orders to move to St Jean, where they arrived shortly before lunch.

They took formal occupation of the buildings allotted to them, and then had lunch, after which they returned, anxious to find the direct telephone line so that they might discover from London exactly what was happening.

Air Vice-Marshal Yool says, 'The main building and its surroundings were in a state of chaos, lorries arriving with cupboards, papers and various stores, and being unloaded, with crowds of men bustling in and out of the building and getting in each other's way with their loads. No one seemed to be in control and confusion appeared to be general.

'Eventually we found our way into a large room where the telephone exchange was in process of being installed. The room was a mass of wires, with numerous excitable Frenchmen dashing about in seemingly uncontrolled disorder.

'The prospects of establishing communication with the Air Ministry from the midst of this chaos appeared remote, but at length we spied a little corporal in French Air Force uniform who seemed to be in charge of the proceedings. Approaching him we inquired tentatively about our line. At first our French did not seem to make much impression, but suddenly a look of comprehension dawned on his face.

'He produced a portable field telephone of extremely ancient pattern and dashed into the maze of wires, which to us looked as though they were in inextricable confusion. Seizing two of the wires he clipped his ancient instrument to them and turned the handle vigorously. Then turning to us with a look of triumph on his face, he shouted 'Air Ministree', and gave me the instrument.

'A miracle had happened.'

For others at home it was a day of harder work than many working days had ever been. Mrs Mabel Hamilton recalls, 'We sat down to our dinner round about the usual time, one-thirty, and had hardly started when a neighbour opposite came across to say that Vickers of Weybridge wanted my husband on the phone as soon as possible.

'He got the car out at once and drove to our business, I wanted no more dinner, so just cleared the table, and when I had almost finished washing up, I heard a knock at the front door. The gentleman who stood there said he was from

St Peter's Hospital and must see my husband at once. It was very important.

'I told him where he could find him and he at once drove away. About twenty-past five my husband returned to tell me what had happened, and also that he could not stay. This is what he told me.

'He had got on the phone to Vickers as requested and taken down the particulars of an order which they required to be delivered at once. He was making out the order when the phone rang and the Matron at the clinic asked if he could bring down as much coal tar soap as he could as soon as possible, as some of the evacuee children were filthy. Would he also take some black paint for the blackout. Then the gentleman from St Peter's arrived and wanted baths installed during the coming week for the use of doctors and nurses who were arriving the next day from Guy's hospital, in London.

'My husband then drove down to the clinic and while getting the goods out of the car, the doctor at the clinic asked him to drive three ladies to their billets (all of them were pregnant.) After that he had come home to tell me he was then going to pick up the plumber to take him up to St Peter's to measure up the pipes and so on, and check up on positions and fittings.

'This was his kind of service all through the war years. I honestly believe if any of the factories, Vickers, hospitals and all the Ministries he served had wanted a pennyworth of tacks in the middle of the night, he would have delivered them without one single moan. Unfortunately there are no medals for this kind of service. Before the war was over, he was ill with angina and died in 1953, as a direct result of overwork during the war.'

As Mr Hamilton was telling his wife what he had been doing and still had to do, Winston Churchill was leaving his flat for the Admiralty to do battle with an enemy whom he had met before.

162

5

Act III - Evening

AT THE VERY moment that Winston Churchill was mounting the steps of the Admiralty, over every loud-speaker in Britain came the strains of the National Anthem. When they had died away, the voice of the chief announcer said, 'His Majesty the King.' There was a slight pause and then came the measured, firm tones of the father of the British family of nations.

He gave to his people a message that was stirring in its simplicity, and for many who heard it, it provoked the first conscious emotional response of the day.

From where she was sitting listening to the King, Mrs Mary Ireland could 'see a small jag of wall-paper about half an inch square, which had been torn away from the wall and hung down behind the wireless cabinet.

'Now, I had seen that footling little piece of loose wall-paper,' she says, 'most days for quite a year, but I suddenly decided it must be pasted back into position.

'I went to the studio and collected a tube of paste, my palette knife and a clean cloth, and there and then repaired the tear with meticulous care so that one could see no no damage at all. Why I felt that it was essential at that moment to repair that stupid bit of paper I have never understood, but I suppose there is some psychological explanation.'

When the news bulletin was read after his Majesty's speech, the more observant noticed that the names of the German and Italian leaders were referred to for the first time without the courtesy prefixes of *Herr* and *Signor*.

One of the most disappointed men on this day was the Italian dictator. He would dearly have liked to support his

German friend by declaring war on France and Great Britain but he was totally unprepared to wage a war of any kind, and his people were praying that he should not involve them.

But it was humiliating, and he tried to console himself with the thought that before the end, he would be ready and in a position to lay claim to some of the spoils.

Hitler, too, had been disappointed that Mussolini had had to declare his country non-belligerent; nevertheless, a non-belligerent ally could still be of some use, if it remained an ally. As a measure to assure this, before he set off for his operational headquarters at the front in his special armoured train, he sat down and wrote to Mussolini a letter in which he said among other things:

'You assured me recently that you believe you may be able to help in some fields. I accept this in advance with sincere thanks. But I believe, also, that even if we should now march down separate paths, destiny will still bind us to one another. If National Socialist Germany were to be destroyed by the Western democracies, the future which Fascist Italy would face would also be hard. I have always felt that the future of our two régimes is bound up together, and I know that you, Duce, hold exactly the same opinion.'

It was a warning, and when Mussolini received it by telegraph two hours later, he recognized it to be such; and though there were to be times in the years ahead when he was tempted to kick against the Nazi pricks, he was never to forget it.

There was another man, too, whose friendly disposition towards him Hitler was anxious to keep for the time being. In fact, at this moment he wanted Josef Stalin's active assistance.

So before he, too, set out for the front in his special train —though why a Foreign Minister should be required at the front it is difficult to explain—at ten minutes to seven, Joachim Ribbentrop sent off to Count von der Schulenburg, Germany's Ambassador in Moscow, a most secret telegram, which the Ambassador himself was to decode, and no other.

164

The Ambassador was instructed to invite Stalin to join in the attack on Poland.

Ribbentrop telegraphed: 'We definitely expect that we shall have decisively defeated the Polish Army in a few weeks. We should then keep the territory that was fixed at Moscow as a German sphere of interest under military occupation. Naturally, however, for military reasons, we should have to continue to take action against such Polish military forces as are at that time located in the Polish territory belonging to the Russian sphere of interest. Please discuss with Molotov immediately and see if the Soviet Union does not consider it desirable for Russian forces to move at the proper time against Polish forces in the Russian sphere of interest . . .'

Now that there were enemies in the West, as well as an opponent in the East, it was essential that the conflict in the East should be concluded as quickly as possible, so that a struggle on two fronts could be avoided, should France and Britain attack at once.

Stalin was only too ready to comply.

While Hitler and Ribbentrop were engaged in composing their respective warning and invitation, there was taking place in Cambridge one of those acts which place the common man above the Princes of the World.

The community of German refugees in this ancient university town were used to holding their Sunday evening service in Holy Trinity Church, after Anglican evensong. Because of the black-out regulations, which had come into force at the same time that the Government had ordered evacuation and the issue of gas-masks, on this Sunday the holding of the service would not be possible.

Since the Anglican evensong could be held before darkness set in, the German pastor went to the Vicar of Holy Trinity, and asked him what he thought of letting the Germans join with the Anglicans.

The Vicar agreed at once, and so it came about that a few hours after the declaration of war, English and Germans, official enemies, joined in a united service, praying, singing and preaching in both languages.

The black-out was to prove one of the major curses of the war from the beginning to the end. It was responsible for more quarrels than almost anything else; it caused countless accidents; though it also provoked many an hilarious moment.

James Percival had driven to his honeymoon in the black-out. He had been married in Manchester Cathedral at noon the day before, and after the reception had set out for Kendal by motor-car. It was dark before he and his wife had reached half-way.

'It was almost midnight before we arrived,' says Mr Percival, 'and I believe few people had such a hazardous start to married life as we had.'

John MacFarlain, who now lives at Port Augusta, in Southern Australia, was in a small village in the Isle of Wight with his family on the day war broke out.

'During the afternoon,' he writes, 'we religiously prepared our little pastoral windows against exposing the slightest ray of light to the German Air Force. I was to return to London to my job that evening, but before I set out I helped to put up the curtains and check their effectiveness.

'Darkness had scarcely fallen when there was a knock at the door. It was Mr Wardroper, the local warden. He called me outside and pointed to a small hole approximately the size of a large pinhead, right up under the eaves. I swallowed my annoyance at his too strict observance of the regulations, and covered the offending hole.

An hour later I was on the mainland in a train leaving Portsmouth for London, in pitch black darkness, alone in my compartment. At the next dimly lit station two young women and a man joined me. The man smoked a pipe and was quiet; the girls whispered to one another. The train rattled on.

'About a mile or so from Eastleigh, I got the shock of my life. On the right-hand side of the track stood a factory as brilliantly lit up as Blackpool promenade at illumination time.

'I was furious and could not keep quiet. My pinhole of a crack against this exhibition of light! I fumed my anger

166

at the folk in the carriage, telling them of my wigging from Mr Wardroper. This was sabotage, I maintained. They laughed at my seriousness.

'At Eastleigh I got out and sought out the stationmaster. ' "Oh, that place," he said, "that's a Government aircraft factory and you know what the Government is!" I returned to my seat speechless.'

Miss Gwen Lewthwaite's Plymouth neighbours did not laugh at her infraction of the regulations.

After the Prime Minister's broadcast, her brother had suggested that they should motor down to Cornwall to see their sister, since no one could tell when they would have another opportunity.

Miss Lewthwaite owned a small chemist's shop not far from the dockyards, but lived about two miles from it on the other side of the town. When they got back late that evening from Cornwall the telephone at home was ringing. The police answered, asking her to go to her shop at once.

'It was dark by now,' says Miss Lewthwaite, 'but as I neared it I could see quite a crowd gathered, and a policeman. Also to my horror, I saw that my shop window was a blaze of light.

'I realized it was a serious matter. A kind neighbour was up on steps trying to nail blankets over the window. The policeman told me that the crowd had been very hostile and some had wanted to break the window to put out the light, but he thought he had managed to calm them down. Of course, I had my keys and quickly put matters right.

'What had happened was this. A friend of mine sometimes came in to make up prescriptions for me. She had been in today, while it was still light. After she had closed, she remembered something she had left behind, and when she went back, she had turned on the shop lights because it was always darkish there, at the same time accidentally turning on the window lights. As it was still daylight she did not notice that she had done so.

'She little realized that she had been the cause of having me called a traitor by "helping the enemy". My regular strangers about at that time, and they had been my accusers.

167

customers naturally trusted me, but there were several Afterwards we used to laugh about it, but at the time it was not so funny.'

The Bishop of Chester, the Right Reverend Geoffrey Fisher, was on holiday at Minehead with his family and a brother-in-law, who was Rector of a parish in the Midlands.

On hearing the news of the outbreak of war, both the Bishop and the Rector thought they ought to return, the one to his palace and the other to his rectory.

The Most Reverend Archbishop Lord Fisher of Lambeth recalls what happened thus, 'I drove my brother-in-law back to his Rectory and then went on by myself to Chester. It was dark long before I reached there, and I had my first experience of driving in the black-out with just my side-lights. It was quite a difficult journey and I was very relieved when I drove the car into the garage.

'My relief, however, was short-lived. Going into the Palace, I found that thirty very rough and dirty children from the worst part of Liverpool had been billeted on me. Fortunately, in the absence of my wife, my secretary and another brother-in-law and his wife who had been passing through Chester and called, were successfully bathing them all and getting them to bed.

'I did not stop to moralize about the war. I have always found that when sad things happen, the best thing to do is to carry on with the next duty that presents itself.'

One of the things about 3rd September, 1939, that has deeply impressed itself in many people's memories was the calm unemotional reaction of the majority of Englishmen to the events of the day, so different from 4th August, 1914, when hundreds of thousands had spent the day outside Buckingham Palace singing *God Save the King* and *Land of Hope and Glory* and *Rule Britannia*.

W. Thomas-Ellam lived in Charlton, South-east London, but on this day his wife was in a Maida Vale maternity home waiting for a baby.

'In the evening,' he writes, 'as I went to visit my wife, I had to drive along Edgeware Road. What struck me most was that everyone in sight, and particularly the so-called

168

working-class were *en fête*. Outside every pub and place of amusement, there were swarms of people drinking on the pavements, many drunk, singing lustily and dancing. As I watched them, suddenly I realized it was not so much jubilation that motivated them as the last-fling-before-the-Deluge sort of feeling, a hopelessness.'

This lack of spurious patriotic fervour was noted, too, outside England. Mrs J. M. de Goede, who lives in Rotterdam, Holland, recalls, 'My sister and I intended to make a trip to the Hook of Holland on that day, and carried out our intentions because it would be the last time we should be able to visit the sea until next summer. While in the Hook, we noticed several of our destroyers watching the coast and checking every ship that came in from the sea, which was something very unusual.

'One could sense a tension already, as if something was about to happen. Then in the afternoon, the Dutch lightship came in and sailed into the harbour. We then understood that without doubt something really serious was happening, but it was not until we got back to Rotterdam that we saw the announcements that England had declared war on Germany.

'Although we had been expecting it, yet we were very shocked, and one could feel it everywhere. Everyone was discussing it with grave faces. It was as if a very dark cloud had been laid upon all of us. There was no cheerfulness anywhere.'

While Mrs de Goede and her sister were being thus puzzled, in Rotterdam harbour the brand new motor-vessel *Oranje*—the same on which Queen Juliana and her husband recently celebrated their Silver Wedding anniversary —was preparing for her maiden voyage to Batavia in the Dutch East Indies, with thirteen hundred passengers aboard. As soon as the British declaration of war became known to the Captain, B. A. Potjer, he gave orders for the Dutch colours to be painted on her sides.

Gerhard Werkman, a reporter on the Amsterdam daily *Algemeen Handelsblad*, was with Captain Potjer as he gave the order, and asked him what he felt about setting out on

169

a voyage in such times. For answer, the Master took the reporter into the ship's chart room, and showed him two routes which had been plotted, one through the English Channel, one to the north of Scotland.

'Which route will you follow?' Werkman asked.

'The Channel by day,' replied Captain Potjer, 'because I believe British home waters will be absolutely safe. The Navy will see to that. But if I must go by night, then I shall take the northern route, for I think the U-boats will not go so far north.'

Late that evening the *Oranje* sailed. Not even her Captain knew that she would never see her home port again until six years had passed.

In a café in Mechelen, in Belgium, a little party of friends was gathered, among them Mr and Mrs Boxhmans. They, too, were glum, and Mr Boxhmans tried to cheer them up by telling them funny stories about the First World War. But when he saw that they were laughing at his jokes out of more politeness, he desisted.

Presently he said, 'I have an idea. Let all of us who are here make a solemn promise that we will all meet here on the day war ends. Let's drink to it.'

'We all drank to it,' writes Mrs Boxhmans, 'but unhappily, in a bombing raid in 1944, the café was destroyed, and when the war was over, only three of the seven who had made the promise were still living.'

A feeling of hopelessness, Thomas-Ellam noted. At one time during the evening, the lady who is now Mrs Netta Rosenfeld, felt a kind of hopelessness, too. Today was her eighteenth birthday.

'I was in the bath,' she says, 'when the first sirens sounded that very morning, but in a panic I jumped from the bath into my velvet dressing-gown. Can you imagine velvet on a soaking wet skin?

'Later in the afternoon my boy-friend telephoned to call off our date for that evening, as his mother was hysterical. Early evening found me sitting on the front door-step in a back street in East London, thoroughly fed up—it was my birthday, I was alone, I had nowhere to go.

170

'Presently along came a boy I knew vaguely with three friends whom I did not know at all. They stopped and asked why the look of misery, and I told my tale of woe.

'One of the boys said his mother and sisters were evacuated, his father was on A.R.P. duty, and his house was empty—just right for a birthday party. So I spent the evening of my eighteenth birthday cooking eggs and chips for four boys I hardly knew, being spoilt with chocolates, sweets and soft drinks; and I have never before or since enjoyed a birthday so much. It is one I shall always remember.'

While Mrs Rosenfeld was entertaining and being entertained, Patrick Coke was becoming involved in a quixotic display of patriotism.

'In the evening,' he says, 'I and a friend, both of us twenty-seven, muddled but stirred by some strange patriotism, were drinking cheap cider, then eightpence a pint or less. In our last pub we met a popsie, and when the pub shut all three went to her place.

'Now we may have been muddled about war aims, but about one thing were perfectly clear. Two men into one girl won't go! After a short discussion we decided to toss to see who should stay and who should go, the loser to join the R.N.V.R.

'I lost! I kept my part of the bargain and joined the R.N.V.R. in H.M.S. *President*. I never saw Peter again. He also joined the R.N.V.R. and was lost in H.M.S. *Wren*. I got through with a forty per cent disability pension.'

While Patrick Coke and his friend Peter had been thinking their muddled thoughts and drinking draught cider, Oberleutnant Fritz Lemp in the U-30 had been making the biggest mistake of his life, a mistake which was temporarily to embarrass Hitler himself as well as horrify the entire world.

Shortly after seven o'clock as the dusk was beginning to gather, Lemp was in the conning-tower of the U-30 as it cut its way through the freshening Atlantic rollers, keeping a look-out for a possible target for his torpedoes.

Suddenly he saw a ship approaching, and at first sight it looked like an armed merchant cruiser, a ship of the type

171

that Commodore Doenitz had specifically named in his signal as a legitimate objective.

Lemp gave the order to dive and for action stations. Within minutes the U-30 had disappeared.

Through the periscope Lemp carefully examined the still approaching ship, excitement at the thought that to him had fallen the honour of striking the first blow for the Fatherland probably clouding his judgement. He could not be absolutely certain that the ship was an armed merchant cruiser, but if it was not some kind of warship, why was she completely blacked out? Obviously, she was hoping that her passage would not be seen.

If she were an armed merchant cruiser, and Lemp failed to attack her, he would be guilty of a dereliction of duty; and it was the thought of failing in his duty that settled the issue for the U-boat commander.

He snapped out the orders to attack. Swiftly he manœuvred the U-boat into position and presently gave the order for the firing of four torpedoes.

The first two missed the *Athenia*, the last got stuck in the tube; but the third struck home, and exploded in No. 5 hold against the engine-room bulkhead.

It took all the efforts of the U-30's crew all of half an hour to clear the stuck torpedo from the tube. When this had been done, Lemp brought her to the surface to observe what had happened to his victim.

The *Athenia* was already listing dangerously, while round her life-boats bobbed.

Presently, as Lemp watched, pride causing a smile of satisfaction to play about his lips, a rating handed him a message from the wireless operator. It was the distress signal from the sinking ship. It read: "*Athenia* torpedoed 56.42N 14.05W.'

Lemp knew the name, knew that the *Athenia* was a passenger liner, and as the knowledge that he had attacked a passenger ship struck him, all his pride and his joy suddenly left him.

'What a mess!' he exclaimed. 'But why was she travelling without lights?'

He gave the order to dive and slunk away, probably the most worried Nazi in the world at that moment.

The *Athenia* was lothe to sink; it was long past dawn when she disappeared at last. By that time many of her survivors had been rescued by ships which had answered her S.O.S. When the final roll was eventually called, 112 people had lost their lives, 93 passengers and 19 crew, of whom 69 were women, 16 were children, the rest men.

When the news of the sinking of the *Athenia* reached the Rutherford household in Hamilton, Scotland, all the children remembered their mother's dream which she had recounted to them at breakfast on 3rd September.

Describing the scene that Monday morning, John Rutherford writes: 'Our house was in an uproar when we heard that my mother's premonition had come true. The rest of us were certain that my brother Jim had been drowned, but to our surprise, remembering how worried she had been all day, my mother said, "Not this time! He will be saved!"

'She was right. He was picked up by a destroyer, landed in Galway and arrived home on 5th September. He then took a gunnery course and went back to sea in an armed merchantman, H.M.S. *Manstee,* which was lost without survivors in February, 1941.'

The Duty Officer in the War Cabinet Office that night was Major Leslie Hollis R.M. During the night Major Hollis's telephone rang and he was told by the Admiralty of the sinking of the *Athenia* with considerable loss of life, including numbers of Americans.

'I thought this was dynamite,' writes General Sir Leslie Hollis K.C.B., K.B.E. 'The point that occurred to me was that the Germans would put out some propaganda claim that the *Athenia* was carrying munitions of war, which she was not.

'I rang up various people and one and all told me to go to sleep and not bother them in the middle of the night as the matter would be discussed in the morning.'

General Hollis's assessment had been quite right.

Early on 4th September, the German High Command issued a statement: 'There were no German submarines in the area at that time. It is likely that a British submarine fired the torpedo as a propaganda measure to influence U.S. neutrality.'

This was the line that was to be taken and it was seized upon avidly by the Propaganda Minister, Josef Goebbels, who made use of it for many months to come. The article published in the *Volkischer Beobachter*, the organ of the Nazi Party, on 23rd October, is perhaps, the best example of Goebbels's *Athenia* story.

CHURCHILL SANK THE ATHENIA

The picture above shows the proud *Athenia*, the ocean giant which was sunk by a criminal act of Churchill . . . by the explosion of an infernal machine . . . Nearly 1,500 people would have lost their lives if Churchill's original plan had worked out as the criminal desired. Yes, he greatly hoped that the one hundred Americans on board would find death in the waves so that the anger of the American people, who were deceived by him, would be directed against Germany, as the presumed author of the dead . . . How long will his office, one of the richest in the tradition known to Great Britain's history, continue to be held by a murderer?

Not until the Nazi leaders were put on trial at Nuremburg seven years later was the exact truth revealed, and Germany's guilt admitted.

As this first day of war drew to a close, no one could foresee what would happen. All that anyone could do was to fortify himself with a determination to wipe the wicked men who had begun it off the face of the earth.

As the man whom Goebbels reviled, put it as he took charge of His Majesty's navies: 'Once again defence of the rights of a weak State, outraged and invaded by unprovoked aggression, force us to draw the sword. Once again we must fight for life and honour against all the might and fury of the valiant, disciplined and ruthless German race. Once again! So be it.'

My own thoughts were not unlike these, though not so

eloquently expressed, as, overtired, I waited for sleep to come.

Not long after we had eaten in the middle of the day, Estonian friends had telephoned. They had heard that we were leaving. Did we want to sell any of our furniture?

Our furniture was new and modern in design and much admired. We decided that we might as well part with it as store it for years and then perhaps never see it again. So for an hour or two we had received potential and actual buyers.

When we had sold all but a bureau belonging to my wife—it was a twenty-first birthday present—I got rid of these well-meaning friends, who would have stayed with us, and we turned our attention to packing. At last, with half our belongings stowed in a strange variety of cases and bags, we stopped for the day, and went to bed. By my watch it was ten minutes past one; in England, ten minutes past midnight.

Already it was 4th September—the second day of the war.